Building
Effective
Evaluation
Capacity

Comparative Policy Analysis Series
Ray C. Rist, series editor

Program Evaluation and the Mangement of Government
edited by Ray C. Rist

Budgeting, Auditing, and Evaluation
edited by Andrew Gray, Bill Jenkins, and Bob Segsworth

Can Governments Learn?
edited by Frans L. Leeuw, Ray C. Rist, and Richard C. Sonnichsen

Politics and Practices of Intergovernmental Evaluation
edited by Olaf Rieper and Jacques Toulemonde

Monitories Performance in the Public Sector
edited by John Mayne and Eduardo Zapico-Goñi

Public Policy and Program Evaluation
by Evert Vedung

Carrot, Sticks, and Sermons: Policy Instruments and Their Evaluation
edited by Marie-Louise Bemelmans-Videc, Ray C. Rist, and Evert Vedung

Building Effective Evaluation Capacity
edited by Richard Boyle and Donald Lemaire

Building Effective Evaluation Capacity

LESSONS FROM PRACTICE

Richard Boyle
Donald Lemaire

EDITORS

TRANSACTION PUBLISHERS
NEW BRUNSWICK (U.S.A.) AND LONDON (U.K.)

Copyright © 1999 by Transaction Publishers, New Brunswick, New Jersey.

All rights reserved under International and Pan-American Copyright Conventions. No part of this book may be reproduced or transmitted in any form or by any means, electronic or mechanical, including photocopy, recording, or any information storage and retrieval system, without prior permission in writing from the publisher. All inquiries should be addressed to Transaction Publishers, Rutgers—The State University, 35 Berrue Circle, Piscataway, New Jersey 08854-8042.

This book is printed on acid-free paper that meets the American National Standard for Permanence of Paper for Printed Library Materials.

Library of Congress Catalog Number: 98-40492
ISBN: 1-56000-396-0
Printed in the United States of America

Library of Congress Cataloging-in-Publication Data

Building effective evaluation capacity : lessons from practice / edited by
  Richard Boyle and Donald Lemaire.
      p. cm. — (Comparative policy analysis series)
  Includes bibliographical references and index.
  ISBN 1-56000-396-0 (alk. paper)
  1. Administrative agencies—Evaluation. 2. Executive departments—
Evaluation. 3. Bureaucracy—Evaluation. I. Boyle, Richard, 1955–   .
II. Lemaire, Donald. III. Series.
JF1351.B83   1998
352.3'0973—dc21   98-40492
                                                                    CIP

Contents

Introduction: Building Evaluation Capacity

Richard Boyle, Donald Lemaire,
and Ray C. Rist

In recent years administrative reform programs in the public sector have placed significant emphasis on policy and program evaluation as a central element in the reform process (OECD, 1995). Evaluation is seen as part of "managing for results" which has become one of the catch-phrases of public sector reform.

Substantial effort has been put into building and institutionalizing evaluation capacity in many countries, particularly in the "industrial" countries. There is now up to thirty years of experience in attempting to build evaluation practice in public policymaking and to integrate evaluation and decision-making. Derlien (1990) has described two "waves" in which central governments have introduced evaluation. The "first wave" countries, involved in evaluation from the 1960s, includes the United States, Canada, Sweden, and Germany. In the "second wave," starting from the end of the 1970s, are other countries which have made significant strides in institutionalizing evaluation, such as Norway, Denmark, the Netherlands, Great Britain, Finland, and France.

In the first wave are countries that sought to institutionalize evaluation as a means to improve government programs and initiatives and enhance monitoring. The evaluation efforts during this time were closely linked to planning and program processes. Key stakeholders were the program administrators as well as the governmental officials responsible for designing and implementing pilot and demonstration programs in such diverse fields as health, education, criminal justice, housing, and welfare.

The second wave grew throughout the late 1970s and into the 1980s when the rationale for and applications of evaluation changed. Now evaluation was seen as a tool of public accountability via the budgetary process, a tool to force the reconsideration of existing justifications for

1

policies and programs, or as a means to influence activities at the political level of government. Evaluation became a means of assessing the performance of government against standards and objectives. In this second wave, the parliaments became much more actively involved, even supplanting the program administrators as the prime stakeholders in national evaluation systems. For the parliaments, the evaluation systems became a means of helping to rationalize the budgetary process and ensure high performance by governmental entities. An evaluation system was also clearly understood as a means to strengthen the role of the parliament vis a vis the government by providing a new tool of accountability.

A Working Group on Policy and Program Evaluation has been tracking developments in these two evaluation "waves" over the last ten years. During that period, the Working Group has carried out substantive comparative research on various aspects of policy and program evaluation (Rist 1990a, 1990b; Gray, Jenkins, and Segsworth 1993; Leeuw, Rist, and Sonnichsen 1994; Toulemonde and Rieper 1997; Mayne and Zapico-Goñi, 1997, Bemelmans-Videc, Rist, and Vedung 1997). In the course of this research, it has become apparent that evaluation practice in a specific country or government cannot be understood and assessed without taking into account the institutional context within which evaluation takes place. Institutional arrangements determine whether evaluations are carried out on an ad hoc basis or systematically; and whether and where evaluation plays a part in managing for results.

Members of the Working Group decided that now is an appropriate time to see what lessons can be drawn from this knowledge of institutionalization. This is a particularly appropriate time as a "third wave" of government-led evaluation initiatives can now be discerned. In Europe, countries such as Switzerland and Ireland are building evaluation capacity. Asia, Korea, and Indonesia are to the fore in attempts to institutionalize evaluation. Governments in Africa and Latin America, with Zimbabwe and Colombia being notable examples, are also trying to build and develop evaluation capacity. Much of this work in the "developing" countries is being supported by the World Bank, which recently established an Evaluation Capacity Development Task Force to help the Bank develop a strategy for assisting borrowing countries to develop their capacity to evaluate public projects, programs and policies (The World Bank 1994a).

Intriguing in assessing this developing wave is that this third group of countries are drawing their inspiration from both the experience and early objectives of the first wave countries as well as from the second wave countries. While the parallel for each third wave country is not absolute to that of both first and second wave countries, there are some striking similarities.

For example, like the first wave countries, the majority of these third wave countries are building their evaluation systems at a time of rapidly expanding economies and growing public sector budgets. They are undertaking large-scale social interventions and they are enhancing their formal planning systems. There is a strong desire to improve existing and new programs. Further, there is confidence in the growing quality and integrity of the public service. With such confidence, efforts to build a national evaluation system are not seen as a waste of scarce resources, but to the contrary, as a positive national investment. The optimistic view is that evaluation will come to be seen by public sector administrators and leaders as an effective tool of governance.

In similarity to the second wave countries, countries of the third wave are also highly conscious of financial constraints and the growing pressures of public accountability. This third wave is organizing evaluation systems in response to the need for visible and transparent means of budgetary and management accountability, the requirements for the rationalization of resource allocations within the budget, learning of and then limiting the resources expended on ineffective programs, and demonstrating to taxpayers that the public sector can deliver necessary services.

Admittedly, there are other characteristics of this emerging wave where the parallels break down, both internally and in comparison to either of the two other waves. Consider these six dimensions where any argument for a strong commonality among the third wave countries appears to be a forced fit:

- The development and institutionalization of the social sciences;
- The existence and maintenance of a trustworthy statistical apparatus;
- The existing capacity to staff a national evaluation system;
- The constitutional relationship between the executive and the legislative branches of the government;
- The population and geographic size; and
- The administrative distance from the center to the periphery of the governmental system.

This list makes clear that while this third wave of countries strive to build their national evaluation systems, there are sufficient dissimilarities that work against many generalizations about them as a group. As with any typology, it has its limits.

The primary aim of this book is to assist those countries which are currently building evaluation capacity or those which are reviewing how their evaluation capacity is influencing decision-making. This is not to say that this is a "how to" text book on evaluation capacity development. It is not. Rather it is a exploration of some of the main issues which any government attempting to build evaluation capacity must tackle. We show how these issues have been tackled in a number of cases, but we do not promote these cases as the best or the only way. We believe that each government faces distinct and often unique circumstances, and that they must contextualize the information contained in this book as appropriate for their own situation. The issues set out here are the ones that from experience we have identified as those that must be addressed if evaluation is to be useful and relevant to the business of government. How this is to be done is not so easily answered. We give guidance and indicate what seems to work in some circumstances, but we do not set a prescriptive course of action.

We hope that this book will be of particular interest and use to those charged with promoting the institutionalization of evaluation capacity in governments. This includes those within governments, both in the legislature and the executive, who wish to enhance governmental evaluation regimes. It also includes those in national development agencies, the multinational lending institutions such as the World Bank, and many in nongovernmental organizations (NGOs) all promoting evaluation as part of a good governance agenda.

Some Definitions

Before going on to look at some of the issues we will be covering, some definitions of the main terms we use are needed.

Rist has charted developments in our understanding of the term *evaluation*. He indicates that:

> The development of program evaluation, both in terms of its methodologies as well as the kinds of questions that it could address, has resulted in a clear expansion of what now comes under its umbrella. The first, and still perhaps main, assumption about program evaluation was that it was a means of assessing program outcomes or effects through rigorous methodological means. But the most recent thinking suggests that program evaluation now can encompass the various stages of life cycles of a program or policy—from conception through execution through impact. (Rist, 1990a, 4–5)

Rist indicates that Chelimsky's definition of evaluation captures this expanded understanding, when she writes: "Thus, a reasonably well accepted definition might be that program evaluation is the application of systematic research methods to the assessment of program design, implementation, and effectiveness" (1985,7). He also makes the point that if this definition is expanded to include retrospective assessment of policies as well as programs, then the evaluation function can be applied throughout the life cycle of a government initiative.

Evaluation and *performance monitoring* are closely linked in that evaluation includes the periodic analysis of performance information from ongoing performance monitoring systems (Mayne and Zapico-Goñi, 1997). The difference is one of degree. Performance monitoring is focused on the day-to-day workings of organizations, rather than on the effects of interventions. Monitoring is more concerned with the design and operation of programs and policies, whereas evaluation focuses more on fundamental questions about a program or policy's existence. But in practice monitoring and evaluation tend to shade into each other, and evaluations often draw heavily on monitoring data.

Evaluation capacity and *evaluation practice* are closely connected. The difference is that evaluation capacity refers to the human capital (skills, knowledge, experience, etc.) and financial/material resources, and evaluation practice to the actual "doing" of evaluation. Evaluation practice refers to the definition of the evaluation, the research design, and the execution of the evaluation activity, that is, implementation, results, and impacts on specific public policy. This practice is only possible if you have the supply of "hardware" (in other words, evaluation capacity).

Organizational arrangements refers to the status of the organization conducting and promoting evaluation within the political regime of a government; either in the legislative or executive branch. The degree of autonomy the organization has in the selection of the evaluation agenda; its capacity in terms of resources (both personnel and financial); access and distribution of evaluation studies; and the obligation generated by specific authorities resulting from the execution of evaluation studies, are all elements that define organizational arrangements. They need to be taken into account in assessing the effectiveness of a specific evaluation regime.

Institutionalization of evaluation refers to the establishment of rules, procedures, and organizational arrangements by which evaluations of public policy are produced within a specific government. An alternative description would be to refer to institutionalization as the process of legitimization by which evaluation practice formally becomes part of the decision-making process of government and public organizations. Formal institutional arrangements ensure that evaluations are not simply carried out on an ad hoc basis, and are conducted with some minimal frequency. In this context, evaluation practice can be seen as part of the public policy development and implementation loop. Also, by making the practice of evaluation explicit, some protection is provided from opportunistic behavior by decision makers. Institutionalization at least specifies a priori when evaluation might be done, and for what purpose.

Evaluation regime refers to the configuration of evaluation capacity, evaluation practice, organizational arrangements, and institutionalization. *Evaluation capacity development* refers to activities and initiatives taken to implement an evaluation regime.

Why Build Evaluation Capacity?

Having stated that evaluation capacity development is a central focus of this book, this begs the basic question as to what purpose is served by governments' having evaluation capacity?

Ignoring the answer that "we will do it because so many others are doing it," the basic response is that governments build national evaluation systems because they believe such a system will help them improve their means and methods of governance. A national evaluation system that is understood, credible, and used enhances the performance of public sector management (The World Bank, 1994a). A system that will provide on-going and systematic information regarding the performance of the multiple units and ministries of a government back to those ministries or to the national legislature is a system that can be used to improve public policies.

A central reason for building a national evaluation system is that in the absence of such a system, there is little objective evidence that one can turn to ascertain the consequences of governmental actions and programs. At one level, in the absence of data, anyone's opinion is then as good as anyone else's. Some may have more experience or more familiarity than others, but there is no body of evidence that can be investigated to mediate the multiple opinions, subjective interpretations and assumptions, or strictly ideological beliefs that frame judgments. Governance in such a condition is subject to the pressures and political assaults of those with agendas, uninhibited by trustworthy information.

If evaluation can contribute, on the one hand, to the diminishing of whim and personal agendas in governing, that is, diminish the opportunities in governing to avoid known knowledge, so, on the other hand, it can provide positive incentives and benefits to those responsible for governing. It can enhance the political process and further "democratic gain" by assisting decision-makers sifting through the multiplicity of opinions and information about policies, programs, and projects.

This is not to say that with data, all decision-making becomes logical, linear, and transparent. Not so. Inserting evaluation findings into a political context does transform the message. The filters through which the evaluation findings must be interpreted are different from those of judgments of technical adequacy. The filters are now those of the political agendas of individuals and organizations. The political context may or may not drown out the evaluation message. If it does, so be it—for many messages get lost in the political arena, often for good reasons. But when it does not and there is an interest in listening, objective evidence on government performance can change the nature of the discourse, bring credible information to the table, and challenge the beliefs and opinions that are driving governmental action.

Governments at all levels are constantly facing pressures to act and react. As such, the responsible policy makers continually face questions about the direction, intensity, breadth, and financial and social costs of governmental action (or inaction). It is in this context that we come to the rationale for a national evaluation system. Such a system can play a vital role in governance, for the questions asked and answered from an evaluation perspective can provide information generally unavailable to the policy makers (both in the ministries and in the legislature) from other sources. The answer (even approximate) to the question of whether a proposed policy initiative is likely or not to achieve its stated objectives is of no small import to those responsible for the decision and its subsequent implementation.

In this context, evaluation is a central element of the trend towards what has been described as managerialism or the new public management in many countries over the past ten to fifteen years (OECD, 1995). In governments as diverse as those in Australia, Malaysia, the United States, and Indonesia, a new approach to the management of the public services is being applied. This approach includes:

- Greater delegation and devolution of operational functions.
- A renewed emphasis on strategic management and control at the center of government.
- Clearer definition of performance expectations.

Evaluation capacity development is seen as an integral aspect of this results-oriented public sector management. It is one component of a broader managerial framework aimed at enhancing public sector performance. But this is not to say that evaluation should be seen as a fashion, to be attached to the latest trend such as "new public management" and then dropped as a new trend or theme emerges. Evaluation is a resilient tool that applies across and beyond management fads and fashions. The key point here is that evaluation facilitates public sector development and the more effective management of the public services.

A well-functioning evaluation system can penetrate the administrative and bureaucratic fog that enshrouds so much governmental action. But just saying this can be done exposes immediately the disincentives for many in government to support an evaluation system because of its perceived threat to self-interest, for example, why open myself to outside scrutiny; why expose my program or policy to external criticism; why set up a system where one of the main objectives will be to force me to explain myself? That evaluation is both more than and different from these perceptions is often not seen nor believed.

Evaluation studies are not automatically used in the decision-making process. Hence the importance of institutional context. Our basic thesis is that the organizational arrangements established to create an evaluation regime are conditioned by the specifics of institutional context. In turn, the success of the institutionalization of evaluation is also conditioned to some extent by the details of organizational arrangements used to produce actual evaluation capacity. Institutional "anchorage" plays an important role in matching or harmonizing the supply of and demand for evaluation.

There is a particular tension between evaluation for democratic dialogue and evaluation as a management tool. Proponents of evaluation for democratic dialogue often argue that the institutionalization of evaluation should take place in the legislative branch of governance structure. Here, the focus is on utility. Ensuring that public money is being spent wisely is of paramount importance, with public accountability a key concept. Proponents of evaluation as a management tool would argue for anchorage in the executive branch. Here, the focus is more on implementation monitoring, and the improvement of policies and government activities over time.

From these different perspectives, the assessment of the usefulness of an evaluation regime may vary. For example, a legislative committee reviewing an evaluation regime located in and at the service of the executive branch is quite likely to find that the regime does not meet its particular needs. The executive could reach the opposite conclusion, based on its own review. Both could be right. The basic question, and the one which is addressed in this book, is which type or types of institutionalization of evaluation or evaluation regime is likely to be most effective in meeting the desired purposes set for evaluation?

Such a question is of particular importance at the moment given the changing role of the state. In many countries, people see a vast and intrusive state that is poorly controlled by the citizens it is intended to serve. There is a widespread political impetus for privatization and the increased commercialization of services. The bureaucratic, highly centralized organizations which have long dominated the public sector are no longer seen as apt for dealing with what people sense to be profound changes in society. The implications of these changes for evaluation are being explored by other members of the Working Group (Gray, forthcoming). The importance here is that this changing role of the state has implications for determining the most appropriate type and location of evaluation regime, and sets the context for our discussion of the institutionalization of evaluation.

Setting the Scene for Evaluation Capacity Development— Some Basic Considerations

Before going on to set out the main themes which the book explores, it is necessary to spend a little time setting out some basic issues that affect approaches to evaluation capacity development and evaluation practice. First, there is the issue of the presence of absence of sound data systems. Good reliable data which can be trusted are obviously necessary if sound conclusions are to be drawn from evaluative studies. If such data systems are not available, initial efforts will have to be put into establishing and developing sound data. Second is the question of whether there is a history of social science. Most evaluation practices and methodologies derive from the social sciences, particularly political science, economics, sociology, management studies, and public administration studies. These fields of knowledge set the scene for evaluation studies. If there is no preexisting history of social science which a government can call on in a country, it will be necessary to call on outside expertise and to promote social science disciplines. This issue is related to the third, the presence or absence of a cadre of trained analysts/evaluators. Whether they be based in the legislative or executive branch, internal or external, individuals, or groups, there is a need for a basic cohort of evaluators who are trained in the methodologies and management of evaluation studies.

A fourth key issue is that of the presence or absence of corruption (political and economic). If evaluation is to be used to enhance decision-making and prompt open debate on the effectiveness of government actions, this will best be done in a setting where the various stakeholders interact openly. Corruption means that evaluation studies cannot properly be undertaken, or if they are, the findings are likely to be either corrupted themselves or ignored. The World Bank has given this issue of corruption serious consideration, and is promoting good governance as a means of sustainable development. The Bank characterizes good governance as: "predictable, open and enlightened policy-making (that is, transparent processes); a bureaucracy imbued with a professional ethos; an executive arm of government accountable for its actions; and a strong civil society participating in public affairs; and all behaving under the rule of law" (The World Bank, 1994b). Similarly, the OECD have recently studied the management of government ethics, and identified the key components of an "ethics infrastructure" including an effective legal framework; efficient accountability mechanisms; and workable codes of conduct (OECD, 1996). Evaluation will be influenced by the presence and promotion of good governance and ethics arrangements, in that they create a more conducive atmosphere for evaluation findings. At the same time, evaluation is one of the mechanisms used to promote good governance, in that it can help create a climate where information is more freely and properly used.

We are not saying that governments must have solved these issues or that they are preconditions for evaluation capacity development. If they were preconditions, many countries would not be in a position to even begin to institutionalize evaluation. But it is possible for governments where the infrastructure is deficient to begin the process of establishing them as part of their building of evaluation capacity. So, for example, analysts/evaluators could be recruited and put through a tailored training program. The very process of conducting evaluation studies can lead to the improvement of data systems. Evaluation, as mentioned, is a tool for good governance. However, to be fully effective, evaluation regimes must have these four elements in place, or be in the process of putting them in place. These elements are often taken for granted, but they are crucial for successful utilization of the information an evaluation system can generate.

A further basic issue for evaluation capacity development is that of the *timeframe* needed for institutionalization. Institutionalization does not happen over night, but needs a number of years of sustained intervention. Governments embarking on institutionalization should be aware that they need to be prepared for a "long haul" if they are to arrive at a position where evaluation practice is a formal, recognized, and utilized part of the decision-making process of government and public organizations.

A Framework for Investigating Evaluation Capacity Development

As has been stressed, the institutional context is very important for evaluation regimes, and conditions the expectations surrounding evaluation practice. Institutional anchorage plays an important role in matching or harmonizing the supply of and demand for evaluation.

Picciotto stresses the structural issues concerning the linkage between evaluation supply and demand:

> There is no guarantee that the managers and staff of development organizations (or developing country agencies) will take systematic account of evaluation findings, however relevant. Neither does managerial awareness of the importance of evaluation translate automatically into the requisite organization setup. For evaluation to fulfill its unique potential, a subtle combination of independence and constructive engagement is needed to contribute to professional excellence through continuous organizational learning. In other words, Say's Law does not apply fully: good evaluation does not always create its own demand. Demand must be nurtured in parallel. (Picciotto, 1995: 22–23)

This issue of supply and demand is explored in the report of the task force on evaluation capacity development established by the World Bank (1994a). The task force specify that building effective evaluation capacity for governments should be driven by an assessment of factors that influence the demand for and supply of evaluation, together with identifying the need and opportunities to strengthen the financial and informational infrastructure. As the task force report states: "If evaluation capacity exists but there is no demand for its use, the evaluation function will remain weak. If there is demand but capacity is weak, then again evaluation will not be done well."

This demand and supply link is crucial for evaluation use. As Bemelmans-Videc (1992) states, "recruitment and actual utilization of evaluation expertise will take place where supply of this expertise and demand for it interact." However, as Mayne (1994) points out, this supply and demand model, whilst conceptually simple, cannot be applied in a simplistic manner:

> Considerable evaluation practice, and most evaluation research, is based on a supply-push assumption, whereby the supply of good evaluations is assumed to create a demand for the information, resulting in utilization.... Alternatively, a demand-pull framework would claim that if the demand for evaluative information is made clear, then evaluations will be produced to fill the gap.

Neither of the supply-push or the demand-pull approaches on their own gives a satisfactory answer. Also, to refer to our discussion on purpose earlier, there are different types of demand that impact on supply and utilization. Demand for evaluation as democratic dialogue is different than demand for evaluation as management tool. These differing demands have implications for supply: where it is located, how it impacts on organizational learning; how it is used; and by whom.

Achieving a suitable balance between the demand for and the supply of evaluation becomes a key issue in evaluation institutionalization. This demand and supply framework for understanding evaluation capacity development is set in figure 1.

FIGURE 1
A Demand and Supply Framework for Evaluation Capacity Development

		Evaluation Demand	
		Strong	**Weak**
Evaluation Supply	**Strong**	High evaluation capacity, high utilization	High evaluation capacity, limited utilization
	Weak	Limited evaluation capacity, high utilization of studies produced	Little evaluation capacity, little utilization of evaluation studies

We aim to explore the key issues which governments must consider if they wish to move to the top left-hand corner box, where evaluation demand and supply are both strong and supporting each other. In this situation, evaluation can be said to be fully institutionalized. This supply and demand framework underlies much of the work in this volume. The themes that we explore, as set out below, all relate back to this framework as we explore how the institutionalization of evaluation could provide for an effective evaluation regime where demand and supply meet. Institutionalization is not an end in itself. It is a means to establish an evaluation regime that serves some purpose. What we explore in this book is what has been achieved by evaluation regimes established through different institutionalization arrangements.

Evaluation Capacity Development and Institutionalization— The Key Themes and Issues

The preceding discussion suggests four sets of themes that should be borne in mind when reading the chapters in this book. The first theme is the creation of a balance between demand and supply for evaluation. Establishing an appropriate balance between demand and supply determines the effectiveness of an evaluation regime. A key question here is whether an appropriate balance means working equally on both sides of the equation or whether to focus first on one side of the equation or the other? Related to this theme is the question of vertical versus horizontal strategies for evaluation capacity development. In balancing demand and supply, should the emphasis be put on developing strategies for sectoral evaluation capacity development or cross-sectoral and horizontal strategies at the local level?

A second theme is the exploration of the reasons for the often weak demand for evaluation evident in many countries and at all levels of government. Many studies of evaluation institutionalization focus more on the supply side, aiming to determine what needs to be done to improve the supply of high quality and relevant evaluations and enhance the instruments of evaluation. Here, we put equal emphasis on investigating the reasons why demand may be weaker than expected given a general interest in evaluation as a tool of good governance, and determining what governments and evaluators themselves can do to overcome or counteract weak demand and establish sources of strong demand for the results of evaluation studies.

A third theme is the utilization of opportunities and incentives to foster evaluation capacity development. Traditional implementation approaches suggest developing a rational and sequential approach to evaluation capacity development. But the reality of governmental and organizational life suggests that an opportunistic approach to evaluation capacity development has at least an equally legitimate claim to be considered when institutionalizing evaluation. Knowing how to identify and exploit opportunistic strategies becomes a crucial capacity determinant. In this context knowing what incentives are available to encourage evaluation capacity development is vital. Incentives can be used both to foster demand and to enhance the supply of high quality evaluations.

The fourth theme is the mainstreaming of evaluation regimes into the functions of government. If evaluation is to be as much a tool of government as budgeting or auditing, it must be generally accepted as an integral element in the governance structure. This requires the use of the products of evaluation regimes in the core decision making process of government.

As Vanheukelen (1994) notes:

> First of all, an evaluation exercise must not be an isolated event but should be embedded in a logical chain of policy management in which each and every link is carefully considered. Good policy-making relies on a cycle of consecutive steps: problem identification and formulation of goals—programming—ex ante evaluation—budgeting—implementation—monitoring—ex post evaluation—feedback into policy. If it does not form part and parcel of this bigger whole, evaluation may not only be lacking the right focus, it risks being pointless too.

So, given these overarching themes which we cover in this volume, what are the key issues that governments must consider in their attempts to institutionalize evaluation? Based on its experience of studying evaluation capacity development over a number of years, the Working Group has identified seven issues, set out in table 1, as ones which must be dealt with by governments wishing to enhance the demand for and supply of evaluation:

The questions on the right hand side of table 1 are the questions that we understand governments wishing to build evaluation capacity development are asking. They are the questions that we explore. However, we would emphasize that these questions do not lend themselves to binary answers. Experience indicates that what is necessary are different configurations of evaluation regimes.

What should these configurations be? An examination of the different evaluation regimes adopted over the years, in the context of the

TABLE 1
The Key Issues and Questions in Building Evaluation Capacity

Issue	Question
Anchoring the evaluation regime	Should the evaluation regime be anchored in the legislative or the executive branch, or both, and where within those branches?
Anchoring evaluation capacity within organizations	What are the advantages and disadvantages of (a) centralized versus decentralized evaluation capacity (b) using internal versus external evaluators?
Evaluation coverage	What kind of activities should be covered by evaluation?
Linking evaluation with other public sector functions and institutions	How and to what extent should evaluation interact with budgeting, auditing, strategic planning and monitoring?
Using evaluation in decisionmaking	What are the key domains of use, and how can evaluation utilization be improved?
Professionalizing the evaluation function	To what extent should evaluation be a discipline in its own right, and what skills and competencies are needed by evaluators?
Fostering demand	What are the most effective ways of fostering demand for evaluation activity?

themes and issues outlined, would seem a useful place to start answering this question. As we have stated previously, the purpose of this book is to draw from the experience of countries that have adopted different evaluation regimes over the years. The intent is to draw inferences about the institutionalization of evaluation and the development of evaluation capacity, its utilization, and its role in decision-making.

The book consists of four parts. In part 1, attention is focused on setting the boundaries for evaluation regimes. Key boundary decisions determining the scope of evaluation regimes are decisions on where to anchor evaluation in the structure and deciding what activities are to be evaluated. Mayne, Divorksi, and Lemaire discuss where governments should locate the main decision-making powers for undertaking evaluation studies, namely, decisions on scope, timing, funding, and methodology. In many ways, this chapter sets the scene for the rest of the book. It discusses the interaction between the supply and demand for evaluation in an institutional context, outlining the implications for evaluation demand of locating supply in the executive, the legislature, or in a variety of locations. How to ensure effective demand rather than weak demand is a key concern. One of the main findings is that successful institutionalization of evaluation may require that evaluation be anchored in several places to meet the several market demands in a jurisdiction.

Sonnichsen also discusses the location and anchoring of evaluation, but at the level of the organization or program rather than from a government perspective. He explores the advantages and disadvantages for organizations of developing evaluators within the organization or of using evaluation expertise brought in from outside. He also investigates the relative merits of placing the evaluation function at the corporate level or at the program manager level. The emphasis is on how best to develop evaluation capacity when decisions on the scope, timing, funding, and methodology are under the authority of the organization. He indicates the key issues to be addressed so as to ensure the successful location of the evaluation function in an organization.

Lee explores the boundary issue of determining what activities should be covered by evaluation in an effective regime. In particular, he investigates how *comprehensive* evaluation coverage should be. He finds that in institutionalizing evaluation, it is more effective to aim for comprehensive coverage of a sector than to encourage the devolution of decisions on coverage to the local level and hope that good practice will encourage others to follow suit. Lee also identifies and explores the trend towards more user-oriented evaluations and the move towards a greater focus on program monitoring as significant influences on evaluation coverage in recent years.

In part 2 we focus on the linkage of evaluation and other government activities. Bastoe explores the desirability of linking evaluation with other public sector functions: strategic planning, budgeting, monitoring, and auditing. The concern is with determining the appropriate linkages between evaluation and those functions, if evaluation is to be a mainstream element of government activity. Rather than aim for a strict model of integration of these functions, Bastoe proposes the development of appropriate linkages within a broad performance management framework.

Rist examines the linkage of evaluation utilization and governance. The focus is on the macro level: ensuring that the findings generated by evaluation systems are addressed in the political systems of governments. He explores utilization from two main perspectives: the instrumental use of evaluation in the policy cycle; and the conceptual link between evaluation and organizational learning. He finds that both perspectives bring important insights to bear on the issue of determining effective usage and ensuring balance between the demand for and the supply of evaluation systems. Governments wishing to create incentives for the use of evaluation information in the governance of states need to apply the findings from both perspectives as appropriate if they are to meet the challenge of building effective national evaluation systems.

Part 3 of the study focuses on evaluation capacity building. Boyle looks at building the human resources needed to supply evaluation regimes. He examines what is needed to ensure the supply of a basic cohort of evaluators who are trained in the methodologies and management of evaluation studies. This chapter explores how best to support the professional development of evaluators. Also, on the demand side, means of educating the users of evaluation to demand quality evaluations are identified and discussed.

Toulemonde looks at many of the other resources needed to build evaluation capacity in addition to the human resource. He examines how evaluation demand can be created and enhanced through the manipulation of these resources, such as money and power. He illustrates how by using a combination of "sticks," "carrots," and "sermons" governments can build effective demand for evaluation. In particular, he identifies how constraints and incentives can be used to ensure that evaluations are done, that they are seen as fair, and that decision makers derive positive consequences from evaluations. The role of incentives, both in provoking demand and enhancing the supply of evaluations, is a key theme of this chapter.

Finally, part 4 of the study summarizes the implications for developing countries of the lessons learnt from the industrialized countries experience with evaluation capacity building and institutionalization. Guerrero outlines a strategy for institutionalizing a public sector evaluation function. His main focus is on building evaluation capacity in developing countries, though his comments are largely relevant to most governments intent on developing evaluation. He places evaluation within the broader context of public sector reform, highlights the importance of identifying and meeting the needs of the users of evaluation, and stresses the need to tailor any evaluation model to country conditions. Returning to the overarching theme of the book, he concludes by summarizing the main points regarding the stimulation of and demand for evaluation and the need to act on the supply side to match demand expectations if institutionalization is to be achieved.

Each of the chapters of the book are comparative, in that they draw their findings from the experience of a range of countries and governments rather than being country-specific. Illustrative case studies of specific examples of good practice are contained in each chapter, and particularly illuminating examples are sometimes highlighted in "boxes." These case studies provide interesting examples of actual practice in evaluation capacity development, and highlight points made in the text in the various chapters. There is inevitably some degree of overlap in some of the case studies used in these chapters, given the relatively small number of governments in industrialized countries which have made significant progress in institutionalizing evaluation capacity. But in general where a case is cited in more than one chapter, each chapter looks at it from a differing perspective, depending on the issue under scrutiny.

One other analytical issue should be mentioned. As with other volumes in this series, the case studies here and the issues explored are the product of the interests of the group of auditors, academics and management specialists brought together under the auspices of the Working Group. These have been validated in discussions with international experts in policy and program evaluation[1] and with World Bank officials.[2] But the findings, and any limitations in the study, remain the responsibility of those members of the Working Group who contributed to this work.

To summarize then, this book draws on the experience of governments that have developed different evaluation regimes over the years. It is not our aim to identify a particular model for or an approach to evaluation capacity development. Rather, the aim is to: (a) raise awareness of the issues to be tackled when institutionalizing evaluation, by illustrating what has worked well or not so well in practice in a number of countries; and (b) allow the reader to contextualize this information to best suit their own circumstances.

Notes

1. We are particularly grateful to Jonathan Breul, Derick W. Brinkerhoff, Harry Hatry, Malcolm Holmes, David Tardif-Douglin, Joseph Wholey and Christopher Wye for comments made on early drafts of individual chapters at a meeting in Washington, DC, held under the auspices of the World Bank, 7 November 1995.
2. We received many useful comments and insights from World Bank officials at an Evaluation Capacity Development Seminar hosted by the Bank in Washington, DC, 6–7 November 1995.

References

Bemelmans-Videc, M.L. 1992. "Institutionalizing evaluation: internal perspectives." In J. Mayne, M.L. Bemelmans-Videc, J. Hudson, and R. Conner (eds.), *Advancing Public Policy Evaluation: Learning from International Experiences*. Amsterdam: Elsevier Science Publishers.

Bemelmans-Videc, M.L., R.C. Rist, and E. Verdung (eds.). 1997. *Carrots, Sticks and Sermons: Policy Instruments and their Evaluation*. New Brunswick, NJ: Transaction Publishers.

Chelimsky, E. 1985. "Old patterns and new directions in program evaluation." In E. Chelimsky (ed.)., *Program Evaluation: Patterns and Direction*. Washington, D.C.: American Society for Public Administration.

Derlien, H.U. 1990. "Genesis and Structure of Evaluation Efforts in Comparative Perspective." In Ray C. Rist (ed.), *Program Evaluation and the Management of Government: Patterns and Prospects across Eight Nations*. New Brunswick, NJ: Transaction Publishers.

Gray, A., B. Jenkins, and B. Segsworth (eds.). 1993. *Budgeting, Auditing and Evaluation: Functions and Integration in Seven Governments*. New Brunswick, NJ: Transaction Publishers.

Gray, A. (ed.) (forthcoming). *Evaluation and the New Public Management*. New Brunswick, NJ: Transaction Publishers.

Leeuw, F.L., R.C. Rist, and R.C. Sonnichsen (eds.). 1994. *Can Governments Learn? Comparative Perspectives on Evaluation and Organizational Learning*. New Brunswick, NJ: Transaction Publishers.

Mayne, J. 1994. Utilizing Evaluation in Organizations: The Balancing Act. In F. L. Leeuw, R. C. Rist, and R. C. Sonnichsen (eds.). *Can Governments Learn? Comparative Perspectives on Evaluation & Organizational Learning*. New Brunswick, N. J.: Transaction Publishers.

Mayne, J. and E. Zapico-Goñi (eds.). 1997. *Monitoring Performance in the Public Sector: Future Directions from International Experience*. New Brunswick, NJ: Transaction Publishers.

OECD. 1995. *Governance in Transition*. Paris: OECD.

OECD. 1996. *Ethics in the Public Service*. Paris: OECD.

Picciotto, R. 1995. "Introduction: Evaluation and Development," *New Directions for Evaluation*, No. 67, Fall, 13–23.

Rist, R.C. (ed.). 1990a. *Program Evaluation and the Management of Government: Patterns and Prospects across Eight Nations*. New Brunswick, NJ: Transaction Publishers.

Rist, R.C. (ed.). 1990b. *Policy and Program Evaluation: Perspectives on Design and Utilization*. Brussels: International Institute of Administrative Sciences (IIAS).

Rossi, P.H. and H.E. Freeman. 1993. *Evaluation: A Systematic Approach*. Newbury Park, CA: Sage Publications.

Toulemonde, J. and O. Rieper (eds.). 1997. *Politics and Practices of Inter-Governmental Evaluation*. New Brunswick, NJ: Transaction Publishers.

The World Bank. 1994a. *Report of the Evaluation Capacity Development Task Force*. Washington, DC: The World Bank.

The World Bank. 1994b. *Governance: The World Bank's Experience*. Washington, DC: The World Bank.

Vanheukelen, M. 1994. "The Evaluation of European Expenditure: the Current State of Play." Paper presented at European Evaluation Society conference. The Hague, Netherlands. 1–2 December.

Part 1

Setting the Boundaries
for Evaluation Regimes

1

Locating Evaluation: Anchoring Evaluation in the Executive or the Legislature, or Both or Elsewhere?

*John Mayne, Stan Divorski,
and Donald Lemaire*

Most governments today are enhancing or developing the ability to measure what is being accomplished by their programs. Evaluation studies of programs and their impacts are key tools that can be used. We assume here that the organization or jurisdiction has decided to build in an evaluation capacity. Derlien (1990) discusses the various historical reasons why organizations want an evaluation capacity. Such a decision could be implemented through an administrative policy, legislation, or a constitutional amendment. In this context, we examined experience with evaluation in several countries to see what happens depending where in government one puts the function.

Information on the accomplishments of government programs can be used in a number of ways. Furubo (1994) reports that in Sweden evaluations of counseling activities have been used to spread specified counseling methods to local governments. Investigation of the effects of different social factors on dental health influenced the construction of a new system of dental charges.

In Canada, the Auditor General Canada (1993, 1996) has observed a number of instances where evaluations had made important contributions. Evaluation of a $2.1 billion tax credit revealed that most of the investment was not used to support development that would not otherwise have occurred, contributing to a decision to discontinue the tax credit. An evaluation of Canada's antidumping and countervail rules resulted in improvements to the administration of these measures that involve $2 billion of domestic goods and over 10,000 jobs. The improvements included a public information strategy and streamlined enforcement efforts.

However, a general decision or requirement by a jurisdiction to have evaluation is not enough for success. In building an evaluation capacity, the location in which evaluation is anchored is key, as are the related organizational and jurisdictional arrangements needed to make evaluation effective. The key decisions for undertaking individual evaluation studies include:

- the scope,
- timing,
- funding, and
- methodology.

We define *the location of evaluation* as the location where these key evaluation planning decisions are taken in a jurisdiction (and then within an organization). Thus we talk about anchoring evaluation where these key decisions and hence accountability for evaluation lie, which may not be where the actual capacity to carry out the evaluations lie. The responsibility for planning and managing evaluations of program performance can be assigned to a variety of locations within a jurisdiction. Much of our discussion focuses on jurisdictions rather than a specific organization, although many of the arguments and conclusions can be applied to individual organizations wishing to build evaluation capacity. In chapter 2, Sonnichsen addresses the issue of building evaluation capacity at the organization level.

Evaluation Location Options

A key decision is often whether the responsibility for planning and managing evaluations is to be anchored in the legislative branch of government, that is, with those responsible for making laws, or in the executive branch, those responsible for proposing and administering the laws and related programs and policies, or perhaps in both branches. What are the possibilities?

Executive Anchors: *program managers* can plan and undertake program evaluations of their respective programs; an *organizational corporate staff* group within each organization can be responsible for planning and undertaking evaluation studies of programs within the organization; and *central corporate staff* within the executive (Cabinet secretariats or central agencies such as a ministry of finance or treasury or budget offices) can evaluate the performance of major government programs, of programs which cut across several organizations or of programs which might need special attention.

Legislative Anchors: *legislative audit offices* can undertake performance audits or evaluations to assess how well government programs are working; and *legislative bodies* can undertake or commission evaluations to examine what the public is getting for the taxes it pays.

Outside Government Anchors: *universities and research groups*, often the source of evaluation expertise, can undertake studies on the effectiveness of government programs; and *nongovernmental organizations*, including *community and consumer groups* affected by government programs can evaluate the benefits they or their client members receive.

Undoubtedly there are other possibilities. Certainly, as illustrated in Box 1.1, all of the above have been tried by one government or another. If one is to consider establishing the capability to measure the performance of government programs, who should be responsible for planning the evaluations? Who should undertake evaluations? What has been the experience of others in anchoring evaluation in different locations? These are the questions addressed in this chapter.

Before proceeding further, let us define the terms we are using.

A *program* is a set of government activities with a common purpose.

Program *performance* refers to the continued relevance of government programs, the results they are producing or their cost-effectiveness.

Program *results* are any of the consequences of the activities of a program. Results cover *outputs* (goods and services produced directly by program staff), *intermediate outcomes* (typically direct benefits to client groups, including client satisfaction) and *ultimate outcomes* (the further impacts on the client group or society as a result of the outputs and benefits being produced).

We are using a quite traditional definition of evaluation, defining it in terms of the process involved, rather than the purpose served. And in those terms it sounds rather straightforward. However, as we will discuss, institutionalized evaluation gets assessed not by the process its follows but by what it produces and how it is used. These considerations make evaluation a very complex organizational phenomena. We will explore evaluation from the perspective of what it addresses and who uses the results.

Box 1.1: Various Approaches to Institutionalizing Evaluation Terminology

Box 1.1: Various Approaches to Institutionalizing Evaluation

Australia. The conduct of evaluations is anchored in the executive branch mainly with program managers. Government is organized into portfolios, which consist of all departments and agencies that report to ministers. Government policy gives responsibility for evaluation to individual portfolios. Arrangements within portfolios for evaluating programs varies. The Department of Finance monitors evaluation plans and monitors and reviews certain evaluations. The legislative branch, through the Auditor General, reviews the operation and effectiveness of evaluation. (Auditor General of Canada 1993, p. 263)

Canada. Evaluation is the responsibility of the executive branch. Government policy gives deputy heads of departments the responsibility for ensuring that their programs are evaluated. The policy calls for the establishment of an evaluation capacity, and evaluations that fall under the policy are often conducted by specialized corporate evaluation units. The policy and the coordination and monitoring of evaluation is the responsibility of the Treasury Board Secretariat a central government agency. Legislation gives the Auditor General, who reports to Parliament, responsibility for reporting on the adequacy with which evaluation responsibilities are carried out. (Auditor General of Canada 1993, p. 241)

United Kingdom. The primary responsibility for evaluation is with the executive branch. Government policy gives each department responsibility for evaluating its programs. Within departments, evaluations may be carried out by corporate staff, including specialized units, or program managers. Although the Treasury, a central agency, provides central advice and guidance, there is no separate agency responsible for monitoring the implementation of evaluation. The National Audit Office can examine departmental evaluations and can conduct effectiveness audits, giving a partial anchor for evaluation in the legislative branch. (Auditor General of Canada 1993, p. 265)

United States. Evaluation is anchored in both the legislative and executive branches. Evaluations are conducted by both government departments and agencies, and by the General Accounting Office, the legislative auditor.

France. Decisions regarding which policy evaluations to undertake at a corporate government level are made within the executive branch by the Inter-Ministerial Committee of Evaluation, a committee of ministers, chaired by the Prime Minister. The Committee makes its decisions in response to requests from cabinet members and other government agencies, including the legislative audit office, the Cour des Comptes. An independent Scientific Council on Evaluation advises the Inter-ministerial committee on methodology and on the quality of completed evaluations and funding is through a third body, the National Fund for the Development of Evaluations. Other evaluations are undertaken within ministries or independent state agencies such as the National Committees of the Evaluation of Universities or Evaluation of Research. (Cretin 1991, Nioche 1992)

Finally, we refer to a *corporate government* group or unit as one location for evaluation. By this we mean an organization at the center of government such as a ministry of finance, a treasury office, a prime minister's office or other such central agency with responsibilities for government-wide matters.

Considerations in Anchoring the Evaluation Regime

Many kinds of evaluations are undertaken to address a wide range of issues concerning the performance of a program. Also, a wide range of individuals or groups use evaluation findings. This diversity is at the heart of the problems encountered in undertaking effective evaluation: there is no single thing called evaluation and each evaluation study is a unique enterprise. Furthermore, once completed, most evaluations are available for use by a variety of interested parties.

Table 1.1 below identifies four general categories of evaluation users and their differing information needs. The categories and information needs are not completely mutually exclusive nor exhaustive but rather serve to highlight the major differences that need to be considered when planning for an evaluation function.

What is of importance to us is the fact that no single evaluation, or as we will argue, no single evaluation function, can practically handle all of the information identified in table 1.1. To do so would require a mammoth and unmanageable data collection and analysis effort with which few would be satisfied. Experience suggests that *evaluation studies need to be reasonably well-focused and specific to be useful, and that the location of evaluation significantly influences the focus it takes.*

Indeed, there is a large component of professional evaluation devoted to the discussion of and development of ways of scoping an evaluation so that it is useful. Evaluability assessment (Rutman 1980, Wholey 1983) and evaluation assessment (Corbeil 1992, Office of the Comptroller General 1981) are approaches discussed in the literature for focusing evaluations. Patton (1980[1]) stresses the importance of scoping evaluations through involvement of the stakeholders involved to make the studies useful and practical.

We can see that, in deciding where to anchor evaluation (i.e., who is going to decide the scope, timing, funding and methodology of the evaluations), two critical strategic questions need to be considered: Which evaluation issues are to be addressed? and Who is going to use institutionalized evaluations?

TABLE 1.1
Users and Information Needs

User Type	Specific User	Examples of Performance Information Needs
Program User	Front-line program deliverers	Are the right procedures being followed? Are the clients being served well? Are they satisfied? Are operational delivery targets being met?
	Program management	Is service being effectively delivered? Is the program being delivered as efficiently as possible? Are the immediate program objectives being met?
Staff/ Executive User	Corporate management in the organization	Are the program objectives being met? Are the right resources being applied? Is the problem being addressed still a problem? Is the program consistent with the organization's current mission?
	Ministers, Ministries, corporate government staff	Are the program objectives being met as efficiently as possible? Is the program consistent with current government priorities? Can we continue to afford the program? Should government still be in this business?
Legislative User	Legislatures and their committees	How are the program benefits distributed among the public? Are the program objectives being met and providing value for money? Are prudence and probity observed in delivery of the program? Is this an appropriate role for government? Are the right policy instruments being applied?
	Legislative audit bodies	How good is the performance information used? Are the program objectives being met and providing value for money? Being delivered efficiently? Are prudence and probity observed in delivery of the program?
Public User	The public (including consumer and community groups)	Is quality service being provided? Is value for tax dollars being obtained? Are prudence and probity observed in delivery of the program?
	Non-Government Organizations	Are the intended benefits being received by the intended target group? Is the program appropriately resourced?
	Research communities	Is the program intervention working? What is the body of research saying about this type of intervention?

We will discuss each of these considerations and some of the key issues raised in light of the experience gained. We will then look at the implications of anchoring evaluations in each of the executive and legislative locations listed earlier. We will summarize these findings in terms of the 'market' for evaluation information and then address several tactical and practical issues.

Which Evaluation Issues are to be Addressed?

Improving Programs or Challenging Them?

The information of interest to users of evaluations identified in table 1.1 ranges from questions about specific operational activities, to questions about the extent to which the program is accomplishing what was intended and to questions about the program's role in society. These questions range from being relatively straightforward to measure to presenting quite difficult analytical challenges. Further, they range from very operational to rather political.

For our purposes it will be useful to distinguish between three different types of such issues: those that deal with the operations of programs, those which question the success of the program and its delivery approach and those which examine more fundamental issues about the continued need of the program. Table 1.2 outlines these key distinctions.

Different locations are better suited to dealing with each of these classes of issues. As suggested in the comments in table 1.2, as we move from operational issues to impact issues to rationale issues, evaluations become more challenging in terms of organizational resistance. The move from operational to impact issues also entails challenging technical difficulties. Assessing success is more difficult than questions regarding program operations. Determining the continuing need for a program is the most challenging question of all. Evaluation regimes quite often will address operational performance issues well. They are usually easier to measure and analyze, are of immediate interest to those close to the program who may control access to the program and its information, and speak directly to questions of *improving* the program rather than *challenging* its existence.

Dealing With Impact and Relevance Issues

Assessing a program's impact and its continued necessity can be a

TABLE 1.2
Classes of Evaluation Issues

	Typical Issues	Comments
Operational Issues (dealing with work processes, outputs and benefits produced, inputs used)	Are operating procedures efficient, effective and appropriate? Are operational objectives being met?	• are generally easier to measure • deal with performance matters more under the control of the program management • for the most part, deal with issues of direct interest for ongoing management
Impact Issues (dealing with benefits and outcomes produced, organizational capacity)	Are the intended outcomes being achieved? Are there better alternative ways of delivering the services? Will the program continue to produce the intended outcomes?	• are often more difficult to measure • are under less control by program management • assume the continued existence of the program
Continued Relevance Issues (dealing with the future of the program: continued relevance, rationale, future directions, funding)	Is the program still needed? Is the program consistent with current government priorities? Can the program be afforded in light of other priorities? Are their better alternative programs to achieve the objectives?	• challenges the continued existence of the program • deal with issues of direct interest to oversight and funding parties

challenge. How to get institutionalized evaluation in a jurisdiction or organization to address these evaluation issues has proven to be difficult. These are the more fundamental and threatening questions about the well being of organizations and their programs, and are posed more often by those outside the organization (Johnson 1992). They tend to challenge the status quo, challenge the ways things are being done and challenge peoples' jobs. In addition, to get credible evidence on impact issues require more sophisticated measurement practices. In general, the closer that evaluation is located to the program, the more difficult it is to address impact and relevance issues.

These issues relate to questions of double-loop learning, as discussed in a previous book in this series edited by Leeuw, Rist, and Sonnichsen (1994) and are at the heart of the question of where to locate evaluation practice in an organization. True learning organizations (Wildavsky 1985) are rare, so that institutionalizing this form of evaluation requires strong leadership and corresponding cultural change, from within the organization or strong direction from outside the organization.

We suggest that a *major challenge for institutionalized evaluation is to adequately address impact and continued relevance issues.*

Yet, as we will see in the next section, these issues are often assumed by many users of and commentators on evaluation to be key issues for institutionalized evaluation to deal with.

Operational evaluation issues, on the other hand, are usually met with much less resistance in organizations, and indeed are to some extent addressed in all organizations. Managers need information on operational performance to get on with their job and, hence, sometimes with help from an internal evaluation group, tend to have or want this type information available and to use it. Thus measurement of operational issues tends to take place within the program concerned and certainly within the organization, and this seems quite appropriate. Difficulties often arise, however, when an internal evaluation capacity is expected to also deal with continued relevance and certain impact issues (Johnson 1992).

Table 1.3 summarizes the experience of many countries with the kind of performance information that is produced by evaluation capacity in different locations. Box 1.2 provides specific experience from several jurisdictions illustrating the conclusions in different cells of table 1.3.

A key conclusion is that t*he closer the evaluation anchor is to the program, the less likely is it able to deal adequately with continued rationale and impact issues.*

Evaluation anchored close to programs faces a variety of pressures to not too vigorously challenge the basic rationale and success of programs:

- the need for cooperation from the program staff and management to assist in providing good operational data,
- the need to be seen as useful to the organization
- the unwillingness for strategic issues to be addressed by the management.

There is also the very real practical difficulty of not being able to step back and look at the program from "outside the box." Independence does often make an objective, outside and more questioning look

TABLE 1.3
The Kinds of Evaluation Information Forthcoming from Different Anchors

Location of Evaluation	Evaluation Issues		
	Operational Issues	Impact Issues	Continued Relevance Issues
Program Manager	• of most interest to managers and their staff • operational issues addressed well	• impact issues may get addressed, at least in part • useful for justifying program • may be avoided if program not working well or information likely to be used against the program	• relevance issue will NOT get addressed (too threatening to the continued existence of the program)
Corporate Group in the Organization	• operational issues of some interest and may get addressed • organizational-wide operational issues will be of interest and get addressed	• impact issues should be of interest and get addressed • may be avoided if too threatening	• relevance issues may get addressed if program not too large a component of the organization • major organizational rationale issue will NOT be addressed
Corporate Government Group	• operational issues of less interest, and hence less chance of getting addressed • government-wide operational issues will get addressed	• impact issues of direct interest would get addressed	• relevance issues concerning programs will get addressed if it is in the interest of the government to do so
Legislative Audit Office	• operational issues will get addressed for large programs • organizational and government-wide operational issues will get addressed	• impact issues of direct interest as a value-for-money concern and will get addressed	• relevance issues may not get directly addressed if they are seen as political in nature
Legislative Bodies	• operational issues of little interest, and hence little chance of getting addressed	• impact issues of direct interest and will get addressed • distance from the program data and information may be a problem	• relevance issues likely to get addressed
Outside Government	• operational issues mostly of little interest	• impact issues of direct interest, both impact on recipients (user groups, NGOs) and on the society at large (universities)	• relevance issues likely to get addressed by university and research groups

Box 1.2: What Evaluation in Different Locations Actually Produces

Box 1.2: What Evaluation in Different Locations Actually Produces

Canada. In Canada, deputy heads of government departments are responsible for ensuring that their programs are evaluated (the corporate organization model). Audits by the Office of the Auditor General in 1993 and 1996 found that evaluation managers attached the greatest importance to helping management solve operational issues and improve programs. They placed a much lower priority on challenging existing programs to support resource allocation decisions and on evaluating large program units to support accountability to Parliament.

Consistent with their desire to assist program managers, they viewed non-evaluation work as important in establishing the credibility of the function and fostering the use of evaluation findings. Non-evaluation work included reviewing program management and operations, participating in policy and program development and analysis, and providing technical support such as statistical analyses. Consistent with their priorities, evaluation managers focused their evaluations on operational effectiveness issues of smaller units of government activities or programs. In a smaller proportion of cases, evaluations also contributed to significant reforms that reoriented programs in visible ways and to significant cost-savings.

Mayne (1994, 23-25) reporting similar utilization findings in the Canadian federal government, points out that evaluation has, as a result, been quite useful to program managers. About 40% of the evaluations examined led to modifications in program operations and delivery. Another 10% confirmed that the program was on track. Almost 30% led to better understanding about the program and its operations, although led to no specific change. Finally, about 20% led to significant reform or termination, evidence that some evaluations were challenging programs.

The Auditor General Canada(1993) observed that evaluations contributed most frequently to promoting a better understanding of the programs and their rationale among line managers and clientele and to better information for reporting on program performance. They also contributed to operational changes that improved program delivery, in ways that were not always visible to program clients.

Australia. The Australian approach is closer to the program managers model. A Department of Finance Evaluation Task Force reported in 1988 that evaluation was not well integrated into corporate and budgetary decision making, that most internal evaluations emphasized process and efficiency and paid little attention to program effectiveness, an issue that is key for strategic decision-making and accountability reporting. (Ryan 1992)

Nevertheless, by 1994, several reports produced by the Australian Finance Department (Commonwealth Department of Finance, 1994) stated that close to half of the proposals for new policies and programs submitted to Cabinet were supported by evaluation. It is estimated that nearly one-fifth of Cabinet decisions were influenced by the evaluations

United States. The United States General Accounting Office (1992) has reported that evaluations have made a strong contribution to informed decisions by helping programs survive rounds of budget cuts and contributing to dropping or slowing down programs showing extreme weaknesses.

easier to undertake. All this is not indicative of shortcoming with internal evaluators. Rather, the reality is that internal evaluators will not be interested in issues for which there is little demand, or which the organization does not wanted raised.

Who is Going to Use Institutionalized Evaluations?

Table 1.1 listed a number of possible users of evaluation information. If in a given jurisdiction, only one of those users commissioned evaluations and the findings were only to be used by them, then of course that is where to anchor the evaluation efforts. However, this is not the case. At one time or another, each of the users listed in the table will want to use evaluation findings and conclusions on the performance of programs.

Moreover, the findings are often, in fact, available to some or all of the "other" users in table 1.1. In many jurisdictions, the findings from evaluations are routinely available to any interested party. In others, evaluation findings—or some of the findings—are restricted to the organization or government which has produced them. Nevertheless, a basic characteristic of institutionalized evaluation is that *all this is complicated by the fact that whichever user evaluation is anchored with , there will be others who will make use of the evaluation findings and conclusions.*

Thus, in deciding where to anchor evaluation (what we might call the primary users), considerable thought must be given to the use that is likely to be made or could be made by the other various key players in the jurisdiction. The problem that arises is that other users may not find the evaluations as useful as they wish. Box 1.3 provides some examples of the experience in several countries.

As in many things, quality lies in the eyes of the beholder, and four key factors influence the perceived usefulness of the information: the scope, what gets evaluated, the timing, and reliability.

Evaluation Scope

Inappropriate scope may be the primary barrier to use by others of evaluation. We have seen that evaluations can potentially address a wide array of issues, but must be more focused to be manageable. We have also seen that the user with which evaluation is anchored will be interested in a limited scope of issues. As a result, users other than

Box 1.3: The Usefulness of Evaluations for "Other" Users

Box 1.3: The Usefulness of Evaluations for 'Other' Users

United States. The General Accounting Office is a legislative auditor. Looking at the use made of GAO evaluations in the organizations evaluated, the National Academy of Public Administration (1994) observed that evaluations done by or for the managers of an organization often have a better chance to reach the desired audience in a non-confrontational manner and achieve the support and cooperation of officials who must carry out the needed improvements.

The Netherlands. In 1989, the Dutch Court of Audit conducted a review of policy evaluations conducted within the Dutch central government, examining the extent to which there was a demonstrable, recorded use of these studies. The review also examined whether the users were parliament, ministers or civil servants, concluding that reports were used principally by civil servants and far less by ministers and Parliament. (Leeuw and Rozendal 1994)

Canada. The 1993 audit of program evaluation by the Auditor General Canada concluded that the federal evaluation function did not meet the expectations of Cabinet, Parliament and the public. Evaluations focused on operational matters, and many large expenditure programs had not been evaluated. As a result, more progress was required in developing program evaluation that met these external interests. In 1996, the Auditor General observed that although progress had been made, evaluations still did not necessarily result in the information on overall program effectiveness that is needed to support accountability and government decision making.

Australia. Senator John Coates (1992) observed that "most senators rate the political and information gathering functions of the estimates process higher than the management improvement process for which the evaluation data are ostensibly supplied.

those with whom evaluation is anchored will likely not have their specific performance issues addressed in the manner they want.

Experience suggests that the major criticism by users of evaluations frequently is that the study did not address the "right" issues, in particular, avoided what others see as the tough issues—the challenging strategic issues. Box 1.4 illustrates several examples. In particular, as we go from program management to outside the department to outside the government—what we shall refer to as the organizational/jurisdictional ladder—the interest of evaluation users tends to become more and more focused on impact and relevance issues and less and less on operational issues. Generally speaking, the greater the organizational "gap" between anchor and user, the greater is the likelihood that the "wrong" issues get addressed and the perceived usefulness of the evaluation correspondingly diminished.

Box 1.4: Criticisms of the Scope and Timeliness of Institutionalized Evaluation

Box 1.4: Criticisms of the Scope and Timeliness of Institutionalized Evaluation

Australia. The Department of Finance finds that the quantity and quality of evaluations has increased in recent years, but some problem areas remain. A number of program managers have not been predisposed to ask the hard questions or reveal problem areas when conducting evaluations of their programs. Cases have arisen where evaluations commissioned by Cabinet or planned by portfolios have not been completed in sufficient time to feed into Cabinet decisions. In a few cases, portfolios have quoted selectively from evaluation findings. (MacKay 1994).

The Australian National Audit Office found that devolution of evaluation responsibility within a portfolio and agency can result in a loss of sight of the agency's overall objectives and corporate goals (Taylor 1992).

Canada. The federal government has reported concern with the credibility of departmental reviews, including evaluations, where there is an interest in using these for the purposes of government decisions, accountability and public reporting. This concern is attributed to differences in views on the questions addressed and to the perception on the part of central agency officers that reviews undertaken within departments may sometimes interpret results in a manner that could be considered self-serving. (Treasury Board 1995).

France. As noted earlier, decisions as to which corporate government evaluations will be undertaken are made by the Inter-Ministerial Committee of Evaluation, a committee of the Prime Minister and the principal cabinet ministers. Nioche (1992) observes that the first five evaluations selected by the Interdepartmental Committee for evaluation included areas already subject to much evaluation, did not reflect pressing social problems, nor touched on policy areas that were the object of public debate

Evaluation Entity

Another issue affecting usefulness is just what is being evaluated. The programs which get evaluated may not be those of interest to others looking for evaluation findings and conclusions (Nioche 1992). Equally, the entities which get evaluated may be seen to be either not large enough to merit interest (OAG 1993[2]), or too large and high level to produce findings which program managers can react to (NAPA 1994).

Evaluation in a particular location will tend to focus on entities normally dealt with by that location, or lower level entities. Thus program management will likely focus evaluation efforts on their programs or components thereof. As evaluation is located higher up the organizational/jurisdictional ladder, it will tend to look at broader programming areas rather than single programs or even single departments. This entity perspective interacts with the scope question, since evaluations focused on broader programs are less likely to deal with more specific operational issues, and hence be less useful to program managers. Conversely, evaluations focused on smaller entities may not address the broader issues of concern to central government or the legislature.

Evaluation Timing

Another major problem that occurs when others want to use evaluations is that they may not be available when needed. This is a serious problem with institutionalized evaluation, since the various users listed in table 1.1 will almost always be working to different timetables. Without a great deal of planning, evaluations produced at one location will not be ready when others need them, or will be seen as too dated. Some examples are shown in Box 1.4.

Further complicating this is the fact that the different locations may have different planning horizons or timetables. Many managers and groups find themselves only able to react to events and have to work with short time frames. Others have longer time horizons to plan with. If organizations are undergoing significant changes, evaluations producing findings which do not fit into their change agenda may be seen as not very useful.

Evaluation Reliability

A classic evaluation problem is one of the reliability of the findings and conclusions, particularly when the findings do not agree with preconceived notions about the performance of a program. Again this problem is increased when there are multiple users of evaluations in an institutional setting. Different users are likely to look for different levels of reliability. Evaluation research tends to acquire credibility through the use of accepted scientific practice. However, more rigor usually requires more time with the risk that the information provided will not be timely for the decisions to be made. It also cost more. Therefore, evaluation in support of operational management tends to make do with less rigor, under the assumption that day-to-day management goes on and is better informed with some information rather than none.

Table 1.4 summarizes the kinds of credibility and usefulness problems that arise when use is made of evaluations other than where it is anchored.

We conclude that *when considering where to anchor evaluation, consideration must be given to the intended use by other users of the*

TABLE 1.4
The Usefulness of Evaluations

Location	User of Evaluation Information			
	The Organization	Corporate Government	Legislative Audit Office or Body	Public
Within the Organization (with Program Management or Corporate Group)	• good chance for utilization unless the 'other' group is excluded from design decisions	• usefulness likely a problem: – scope, entity, timing, probably 'wrong' – reliability of unwanted findings will be challenged	• usefulness a problem: – scope and entity may be 'wrong' – need for some form of assurance re reliability	• usefulness likely a problem: – timing of access to findings may be a problem – findings likely challenged as self serving
With Corporate Government Group	• usefulness likely a problem: – scope may be 'wrong' – operational realities may not be seen to be adequately captured	• *usefulness not an issue*	• usefulness a problem:: – access to findings may be a problem – need for some form of assurance – scope and entity may be wrong	• usefulness a problem: – timing of access to findings may be a problem – findings likely challenged as self serving
With Legislative Audit Office or Body	• usefulness a problem: – scope may be too broad – may be seen as 'political' if with a legislative body – program realities may not be adequately captured	• usefulness may be a problem: – timing may be a problem – unwanted findings will be challenged – program realities may not be adequately captured	• *usefulness not an issue*	• usefulness quite possible: • scope may be 'wrong' for some groups – credibility high
With the Public (NGOs, Universities, Interest Groups, etc.)	• usefulness a problem : – scope probably too broad or wrong – operational realities may not be adequately captured – may be seen as political or self-serving if with NGO interest group	• usefulness a problem: – timing may be a problem – unwanted findings will be challenged – program realities may not be adequately captured	• usefulness possible: – need for some form of assurance	• usefulness may be a problem between groups: – scope may be 'wrong' between some groups – reliability may be questioned between some groups

evaluation findings. The right scope, the right entity, the right timing and right level of reliability tend to differ among different users.

There are several steps that can be taken to try and increase the credibility of evaluations to others, to which we now turn.

Enhancing Usefulness

We are concerned about how an evaluation anchored in one location can be used with a reasonable level of confidence by others elsewhere. How can we get the scope, the entity, the timing and reliability "right"?

First as to reliability, we suggest above that reliability of evaluations for some users is not the primary constraint to the usefulness of institutional evaluations; there are usually other more serious problems. The exception might be legislative audit offices and universities. There are a variety of ways that reliability can be enhanced, such as the use of professional evaluators, monitoring, external review and adherence to professional standards. Other chapters in this book address this issue more directly, and to which we refer the reader.

Of more interest to us is dealing with the scope, entity and timing issues, the areas where institutionalized evaluations often fall down (see Box 1.4). The institutional solution lies in the often stated suggestion to increase the involvement of the user of the evaluation in its design. Intended users of evaluations have to make known which aspects of performance they are concerned about and what their own time frame is and be able to influence the design of the evaluation. Taylor (1992) notes that to achieve fair and unbiased assessment of programs requires an interactive balancing of views and interests. This requires, at a minimum, consultation with or involvement of parties external to the program or agency.

In some cases, the evaluation approach or policy provides for this influence by others. This, of course, is not enough. Where they can, users must take advantage of the opportunity. In other cases, the other user may have enough power or influence in the system to insist the evaluation covers their concerns. But even in this case, they have to act.

We suggest that t*o ensure utility of evaluations to various interests, structure and controls are not sufficient. Where they can have an influence, institutional users of evaluation must be proactive and assume responsibility for getting the kinds of evaluations they want others to produce.*

This is not as obvious a point as it might appear to be. It is much more common to find the other institutional users of evaluations expect that a "good" evaluation will surely deal with the clearly important performance issues and be available in time for appropriate decision-making or accountability. They are often disappointed.

But one advantage of institutionalizing evaluation is that a variety of administrative procedures can be built into the system. Thus, getting other users of evaluations to be more proactive and responsible for evaluations can be made a formal part of the institutional process. For example, use can be made of steering or advisory committees which include members from various user groups to provide direction and advice to specific evaluations. Or, the evaluation process can include a sign-off by specific users on the terms of reference of each evaluation to ensure that their evaluation issues get addressed and in a timely manner.

We turn now to using our observations on anchoring institutionalized evaluations to explore the specific implications that follow for the different locations identified in the introduction to the chapter.

Anchoring Evaluation in the Organizations Evaluated

The most common way to locate evaluation is to place it within an organization either with the program managers themselves (Australia) or with a corporate group within the organization (Canada) reporting to the head of the organization or as part of a planning, policy, or review unit. This a popular way to institutionalize evaluation and a number of countries and authors have recommended it (Ryan 1992). Responsibility for planning and conducting evaluation is placed with those responsible for the programs.

Benefits

Because of the focus on operational issues, anchoring evaluations within the organization evaluated helps ensure that evaluations will contribute to the fundamental need for good day-to-day management of government programs and to the improvement of program operations. A major benefit is that evaluations can draw on the knowledge of program management and staff. This helps make evaluations easier to perform and helps enhance the buy-in and hence use of evaluation findings by the program management.

As well, individual evaluations may be easier and less costly to perform for a number of reasons:

- The knowledge that program staff and management have of available information sources will minimize the extent to which evaluations have to perform costly and time consuming collection of original data.
- Information requirements may be less demanding than for evaluations anchored at other levels. The technically demanding impact issues are less likely to be raised and the user is able to partially rely on their existing knowledge of the organization and existing management information systems.

Because the user is closer to the program being evaluated, access to program data and information will be less of an issue.

Program managers and their staff generally have a real incentive to know how well the program is operating. Evaluation which draws on the knowledge of program staff and management and which capitalizes on this interest, will have a greater chance of being used. Genuine interest by program personnel will help ensure a focus on critical program areas and program operations that are known to have problems. Evaluations can help managers find the organizational support or resources needed to improve critical operations and can assist managers to find and implement solutions.

Drawbacks

As we have observed earlier, anchoring evaluation within the organization responsible for program delivery results in an emphasis on operational issues at the level of organizational responsibility at which the function is anchored. Anchoring evaluation within program management results in evaluations that focus on operational issues at the local program level. Similarly, evaluations anchored at the corporate level in an organization will tend to examine corporate operational issues. In both cases, there is the danger of evaluation becoming internal management consulting, with a focus on operational issues. Impact issues, to the extent that they do get addressed will tend to focus on the impact of specific operations or management controls, or in result areas where the management of the program has some degree of control.

The organization is likely to focus on carrying out the responsibilities assigned to it, and not question that assignment. Therefore, issues regarding continuing relevance are unlikely to be addressed. The evaluations are unlikely to challenge the existence of the program. They are less likely to see problems that have not already been recognized by the organization.

Even if issues of interest to corporate government and legislative users are addressed by evaluations anchored within the organization subject to the evaluations, the findings may not be of use unless the results of a number of individual evaluations can be rolled up (Auditor General of Canada 1993, p.248). Without strong corporate government direction and coordination, this can be difficult to achieve.

Evaluations in Corporate Government Groups

Benefits

The primary advantages to anchoring evaluation within a corporate government group lies in the kind of issues that would be addressed. Corporate government groups, such as found in finance, treasury, budget, or prime minister's offices, are usually responsible for ensuring the good management of government as a whole and for developing and assisting to implement government wide policies. Consequently, anchoring evaluation here will result in an emphasis on larger government issues related to improving the good management of government or assisting in resource allocation decisions. These can be government wide operational issues and program or sectoral specific impact issues of sufficient importance to effect government resource allocation or policy decisions. Because of their importance to resource allocation decisions, rationale issues may also be addressed, if there is a receptive environment.

Drawbacks

The challenges facing a corporate government evaluation group are formidable and complicated by the fact that it is also a producer of evaluations. The group would not have direct access to the program knowledge or information possessed by program management, and would have to maintain sufficiently good relations with program managers to facilitate access. At the same time, it would be expected to produce evaluation findings that could be critical of program managers, threatening to their programs or lead to restrictions on their discretionary authority, making access and cooperation difficult.

Organizational managers may be hesitant to accept and implement evaluation findings from a corporate government group because of the lack of detailed "insider" knowledge and because the evaluations would not address the program specific operational issues they would find of interest. As well, corporate government evaluation groups could not conduct all the evaluations that would be needed by program delivery organizations. Consequently, it would not make the same contribution to improving program operations as would anchoring evaluation in the organizations themselves. Some of these problems may be offset by involving program delivery organizations in the development and conduct of evaluations.

Use of evaluation findings from corporate government evaluations by legislative bodies may also be problematic. There may be organizational constraints that would prevent corporate government, as part of the executive, from addressing certain issues that would be of interest to legislative bodies. As well, the information collected by corporate government, although sufficient to support executive branch decision-making, may not give legislative officials sufficient context and confidence.

Also, legislative bodies may have difficulty gaining access to findings. In countries such as Canada, advice provided to elected officials acting in their capacity as the senior executive of government is regarded as confidential. Evaluation findings that form part of this advice may be regarded as confidences and unavailable to other potential users.

Evaluation in the Legislative Branch

Evaluation anchored in the legislative branch is subject to many of the same considerations as evaluation anchored in corporate government.

Benefits

The strength of anchoring evaluation in the legislative branch is that it is much more likely to address issues of concerns to legislators, at the time the issues are current, than is evaluation anchored in other locations. The clearest example of this relationship is the U.S. General Accounting Office which undertakes evaluations requested by the U.S. Congress. In addition, evaluation in the legislative branch would be more likely to address issues the executive branch may wish to avoid. And given the independence this kind of evaluation entails, use by the legislative branch should be high.

Drawbacks

Distance of the legislative branch from program delivery makes it difficult to access detailed knowledge regarding the working of programs, and the level of issues addressed may not be of interest to program managers. Legislative evaluation offices must also respect a narrow line between objective comment on the performance of government policy and programs, and the partisan debate that such information can stimulate. The perception of partisanship would be a serious impediment to implementing evaluation findings.

An approach to dealing with these disadvantages is to anchor evaluation in a body that can serve as an intermediary between elected officials and the executive. A common approach is to assign evaluation responsibility to a national audit office, arming it with the appropriate legislation to facilitate access to program information. However, as illustrated in Box 1.4, the use of an intermediary such as the GAO in the U.S. is likely to be only partially successful. The NAPA study (1994) pointed out that the GAO could never conduct all of the evaluations the government needs. Experience has shown that intermediaries may be restricted from addressing certain issues, especially the merits of government policies (Divorski, 1996).

Institutionalized Evaluation: Satisfying the Many Markets for Information

Evaluation perceived as a process is fairly straightforward, that is, the disciplined and analytic assessment of the performance of programs. We have seen, however, that this definition does not address the key issues involved in putting evaluation into jurisdictions or organizations. The important issues and problems arise when we see evaluation as an organizational process for assessing the worth of programs. We have shown that what should be evaluated by this organizational process and what results to expect from this process are very challenging issues. Institutionalizing evaluation is not straightforward but a very complex organizational, political and bureaucratic question.

The Supply and Demand for Evaluation

Approaching institutionalization of evaluation from a supply and demand perspective (Mayne 1994, 35–39) helps to come to grips with some dimensions of what is at issue. Wherever evaluation is anchored it will produce or "supply" evaluations. The institution within which the evaluation is anchored has a variety of needs for information on the performance of programs. A high use of evaluation should occur when the supply of evaluations meets the demand for information.

However, as we have seen, in examining where and how the supply is produced and which demands it is to serve, it quickly becomes apparent that we are not facing a single "market." In examining the experiences of countries that have institutionalized evaluation, what we see are multiple markets for evaluation, each reflective of users with different information requirements—program managers, corporate groups in organizations, corporate government groups, and the legislative. Each market has its own demand with its specific characteristics and its own supply requirements along with it.

We suggest that because of the limitations associated with any single location *successful institutionalization of evaluation may require evaluation anchored in several places to meet the several market demands in a jurisdiction.*

Institutionalization has to take this into account and consider providing for a multiplicity of markets for evaluation where demand and supply can meet. An evaluation regime designed, for example, to meet the demand of program managers does not have the same requirements as an evaluation regime designed to respond to the demand of corporate government staff. Here too there is a danger—that multiple locations of evaluation will result in evaluation "warring factions," perhaps wasting limited evaluation skills and resources in unproductive competition.

We have argued that what is produced in one market could and would be used by other users in other markets. That this could occur effectively was the belief of the Canadian government when setting up its evaluation regime in the early 1980s (Office of the Comptroller General 1981). The theory was that the evaluation regime could be anchored in departments and agencies and supply the demands from other markets, namely central agencies and the Parliament. The experience in Canada and elsewhere reveals that this is very difficult to achieve.

Even though experience leads us to believe that an evaluation regime should be designed in such a way that each market is explicitly dealt with, that is, evaluation anchored in more than one location to supply evaluation for the different demands, we recognize this might just be a reflection of our current organizational capacity to institutionalize evaluation in a fully integrated way. By approaching it in a segregated way, recognizing this reality, we might at the end achieve a more integrated approach by discovering and understanding how the different markets relate to each other.

Indeed, to the extent that organizations or jurisdictions change their management culture to one of managing for results, a productive sharing of evaluation findings may be more likely to occur. When individuals are seeking out information and facts to manage by, the friction between different evaluation markets in a jurisdiction should be reduced.

Accountability for Evaluation

In a real market situation, the interaction between demand and supply is mediated through pricing mechanisms. Of course, we are using the idea of markets for evaluation for illustration purposes. It is essential not to lose sight of the fact that we are talking about an artificial market. As we have seen, in this market, there is no guarantee that supply will be responsive to a specific demand. While there may be a general interest in or global decision to evaluate, this generic demand for evaluation is not enough.

The supplier of evaluation might be quite autonomous in defining what should be supplied to whom and for what purpose. This is indeed what has frequently happened historically and, indeed, is encouraged somewhat by the evaluation profession seeking independence. More importantly from our perspective, we note that a specific demand for evaluation needs to be generated and clearly made known. To believe that "good management" is a sufficient reason to ensure effective demand for evaluation is a very simplistic view of the world.

We argue that the evaluation regime needs to be based on a sound accountability system that provides for bureaucratic incentives and sanctions to ensure that transactions takes place within the "evaluation market." For *successful institutionalized evaluation, those wishing to use evaluation findings and conclusions must be responsible for effectively and realistically making their specific information interests known in each evaluation study, i.e., for making the evaluations useful to themselves.*

This suggestion will be difficult to implement because the assumption of a supply driven market is much more common: produce good evaluations and they will get used. This is also a more comfortable position for those demanding evaluations, since then little responsibility falls on them. Experience, however, shows that evaluations produced under these market conditions (i.e., with no clear user in mind) will not get used to improve programs, although they may contribute to the accumulation of knowledge about government interventions in society (Lester and Wilds 1990; Weiss 1987, 1988).

Institutionalized Evaluation as a Challenge to Programs

Finally, we have seen that getting institutionalized evaluation to address the tougher evaluation issues of continued relevance and some impact issues is very difficult. There is a general demand for this type of evaluation information. Parliaments often put these kinds of questions to governments, and Government in times of great fiscal restraint look for answers to these kinds of questions.

We suggest, however, that

• *For the most part, institutionalized evaluation in the executive cannot realistically supply critical information about the continued relevance of program unless there is solid political demand for the information.*

• *Evaluation anchored in independent legislative audit offices would likely address impact issues but shy away from continued relevance issues.*

• *Evaluation in the legislative branch would address impact and relevance issues, but likely from a more political perspective.*

In thinking that evaluation might be able to supply this information which challenges the existence of programs, we lose sight of the fact that evaluation is an institutionalized process in a bureaucratic setting. Within the executive, it can only challenge programs if that is really what the executive—that is the political leadership—really wants. The legislative branch can challenge programs, but may not have the patience to wait for the appropriate evaluation study to be carried out. And when this interest occurs, there is usually only time available to look at continued relevance issues, not impact concerns. In the legislative branch, relevance and impact questions are likely to be quite political in nature, and hence might be beyond what institutionalized evaluation can deal with.

Further, evaluation is not decision-making. Bringing about fundamental changes in programs, such as eliminating them or changing them completely using different policy instruments, requires considerable will power by a government. The downsizing of most governments over the past few years has benefited little from evaluation.

This is illustrated in the case of Canada. As we have seen, evaluation in Canada has frequently been criticized for not dealing with continued rationale issues (Auditor General of Canada 1993, Johnson 1992). We suggest this is not surprising since the evaluation capacity is located within departments and agencies. After the election in 1993, the new Liberal government, facing serious fiscal pressures to downsize government, undertook a major Program Review. A large number of the programs and policies of government were subject to a serious challenge as to their continued need. An aim was to reconsider just what the role of the federal government should be in the Canada of the 1990s. The Review resulted in considerable change and downsizing of departments with many reduced by 30 to 40 percent and numerous programs eliminated or shifted to the private sector or other levels of government (Treasury Board Secretariat 1996[3]).

An "evaluation" of the continued need of programs was indeed undertaken, but not by the existing institutionalized evaluation function. The Review was undertaken and strongly driven by the elected ministers through a special committee established for the purpose. This most senior leadership by the government was required to address the continued rationale for a wide range of programs and policies. A similar politically led review of programs was undertaken by the government of the Canadian province of Alberta when they felt a similar need to seriously review the role of government.

Serious challenge to a wide range of programs probably needs this kind of political leadership. Expecting such a challenge from institutionalized evaluation is unrealistic, other than, perhaps, on an occasional basis.

The Need for Realistic Expectations

This suggests the importance of not creating unrealistic expectations for institutionalized evaluation. We have suggested above that we should be realistic about what kinds of evaluations can be expected from evaluation located in different locations. This is part of the story. But there is also the fact that evaluation, wherever it is carried out, does not ensure that all questions about government performance of its programs get answered well. Evaluation tries to deal with difficult public sector issues and problems, and faces difficult methodological challenges in trying to measure the outcomes of programs and trying to determine the extent to which programs have contributed to the outcomes measured. Expecting that evaluations will necessarily provide scientifically sound answers to all the issues it addresses is also unrealistic.

More realistic is to expect that evaluation will be able to provide additional useful information about the problems it addresses; that it will be able to reduce the uncertainty about the issue, even if it cannot eliminate all uncertainty. Evaluation has proven useful in many situations. But it does not replace decision-making by responsible persons. Rather it is meant to enhance decision-making.

We suggest that *creating realistic expectations about the role of institutionalized evaluation will greatly increase its acceptance and success.*

Locating Evaluation: Some Practical Considerations

Based on past experience in institutionalizing evaluation, we have outlined some principles that need to be considered when considering where to locate evaluation in a jurisdiction. We have argued, for example, that the optimal answer is for evaluation to be located in a number of different places to meet the several demands which typically exist for evaluation. We want to conclude with a few observations which will influence the question of location in specific cases.

Where is the Demand Coming From?

We began our chapter with the assumption that the decision has been made to institutionalize evaluation. This suggests that at least one party in a jurisdiction wishes to have evaluation. This a good place to situate evaluation, at least initially. One approach is to place evaluation where there has been some evidence of demand for it, keeping in mind the kind of findings that can be expected from different locations.

However, building an evaluation capacity implies resources and a knowledge base, both key elements of power in bureaucracies. Thus the decision of where to build this capacity can be taken as part of a broader strategy to strengthen a particular organization of a jurisdiction (and then within the organization), which may not be with those who have expressed the original demand. We need to realize that building evaluation capacity in a specific organization adds strength to that part of the jurisdiction.

If evaluation is not located where there is demand, there is a risk that responsibility for evaluation will devolve to where a need exists, unless there is compensating central monitoring and quality control (Taylor, 1992).

Final Words

We have discussed the experience of countries institutionalizing evaluation in the executive and the legislative, identifying the lessons we have learned to date on where to locate the evaluation capacity. We suggest that the underlying lesson that has been learned is to be modest about what evaluation in a given location can deliver. Unrealistic expectations can undermine initial enthusiasm and early progress.

Evaluation can produce important findings and conclusions about the performance of government programs. Indeed, some argue (Mayne and Zapico-Goñi 1996) that the capacity to measure the results of programs is essential for reforming the public service. Certainly many countries are trying to enhance this capacity and evaluation is an important tool for so doing.

We believe that much has been learned and countries planning to build an evaluation capacity can benefit from this experience.

References

Auditor General of Canada. 1993. *Annual Report to the House of Commons*. Ottawa.

Auditor General of Canada. 1996. *Annual Report to the House of Commons*. Ottawa.

Coates, J.C. 1992. Parliamentary Use of Evaluation Data in Program Performance Statements. *Australian Journal of Public Administration*, Vol. 51, No.4.[4]

Corbeil, R. C. 1992. Evaluation Assessment: A Case Study of Planning and Evaluation. In J. Hudson, J. Mayne, and R. Thomlison (ed.). *Action-Oriented Evaluation in Organizations: Canadian Practices*. Toronto: Wall & Emerson.

Commonwealth Department of Finance. April, 1994. *The Use of Evaluation in the 1993–94 Budget. Department of Finance Discussion Paper. Canberra*.[5]

Cretin, M. 1991. France. *In Collected Papers from the Second Public Sector Conference of the Fédération des Experts Comptables Européens (FEE): Measuring Performance in Public Sector Management* . London: The Chartered Institute of Public Finance and Accountancy.[6]

Derlien, H.-U. 1990. Genesis and Structure of Evaluation Efforts in Comparative Perspective. In R. C. Rist (ed.). *Program Evaluation and the Management of Government: Patterns and Perspectives across Eight Nations*. New Brunswick: Transaction Publishers.

Divorski, S.W. 1996. Differences in the Approaches of Auditors and Evaluators to the Examination of Government Policies and Programs. *New Directions for Evaluation, Vol. 71. San Francisco: Jossey-Bass*.

Furubo, J.E. 1994. Learning from Evaluations: The Swedish Experience. In Leeuw, F.L. et al. (eds.). *Can Government Learn: Comparative Perspectives on Evaluation and Organizational Learning*. New Brunswick, NJ. Transaction Publishers.

General Accounting Office. 1992. Why Program Evaluation is Important. *New Directions for Evaluation Vol. 55.* San Francisco: Jossey-Bass.

Johnson, A. W. 1992. *Reflections on Administrative Reform in the Government of Canada 1962–1991* . Office of the Auditor General.

Leeuw, F. L., Rist, R. C., and Sonnichsen, R. C. 1994. *Can Governments Learn? Comparative Perspectives on Evaluation and Organizational Learning.* New Brunswick, N.J.: Transaction Publishers.

Lester, J. P. and L. J. Wilds. 1990. The Utilization of Public Policy Analysis: A Conceptual Framework. *Evaluation and Program Planning* 13: 319.

Mayne, J. 1994. Utilizing Evaluation in Organizations: The Balancing Act. In F. L. Leeuw, R. C. Rist, and R. C. Sonnichsen (eds.). *Can Governments Learn? Comparative Perspectives on Evaluation & Organizational Learning.* New Brunswick, N. J.: Transaction Publishers.

Mayne, J. and Zapico-Goñi, E. (eds.). 1996. *Monitoring Performance in the Public Sector: Future Directions from International Experience.* New Brunswick, NJ: Transaction Publishers.

Mackay, K. 1992. Federal Initiatives: the Evolution of Evaluation in the Commonwealth Government. In *Improving Program performance and Decision Making.* Australian Department of Finance. Parkes ACT: Australia. pp. 9–17.[7]

Mackay, K. 1994. The Australian Government's Evaluation Strategy: A Perspective from the Centre. *The Canadian Journal of Program Evaluation,* 9(2), 1994. Calgary: University of Calgary Press.

National Academy of Public Administration. 1994. *The Roles, Mission and Operation of the U.S. General Accounting Office.* Committee on Governmental Affairs United States Senate. Washington. U.S. Government Printing Office.

Nioche, J.P. 1992. Institutionalizing Evaluations in France: Skating on Thin Ice?. In Mayne, J. Bemelmans-Videc, M.L. Hudson, J. and Conner, R. *Advancing Public Policy Evaluation: Learning from International Experiences.* Amsterdam: North-Holland.

Office of the Comptroller General. 1981. *Guide on the Program Evaluation Function in Federal Departments and Agencies.* Ottawa: Supply and Services Canada.

Rutman, L. 1980. *Planning Useful Evaluations: Evaluability Assessment.* Beverly Hills: Sage Publications.

Ryan, B. 1992. Evaluation in the Commonwealth Government: A Critical Appraisal. In O'Faircheallaigh, C. and Ryan, B. *Program Evaluation and Performance Monitoring.* MacMillan, South Melbourne, Australia, p 65.

Sedgwick, S. 1992. Encouraging Evaluation in the Australian Budget Sector. In J. Mayne et al. (eds.) *Advancing Public Policy Evaluation: Learning from International Experience.* Elsevier Science Publishers, pp. 37–48.[8]

Taylor, J. C. 1992. Public Accountability Requirements. *Australian Journal of Public Administration,* Vol. 51, No. 4.

The World Bank. 1994. *Evaluation Capacity Development.* Report of the Task Force. July 5.

Treasury Board Canada 1995. *Strengthening Government Review: Annual Report to Parliament by the President of the Treasury Board on the Performance of Review.* Ottawa.

Treasury Board Canada. 1996. *Program Expenditure Detail: A Profile of Government Spending.* Supply and Services: Ottawa.

Weiss, C. H. 1997. Research for policy's Sake: the Enlightenment Function of Social Research. *Policy Analysis* 3, no. 4, 531–45.

Weiss, C. H. 1988. Evaluation for Decisions: Is Anybody There? Does Anybody Care? *Evaluation Practice* 9 February: 5–19.

Wholey, J. 1983. *Evaluation and Effective Public Sector Management.* [9]Little & Brown.

Wildavsky, A. 1985. The Self-Evaluating Organization. In E. Chelimsky (ed.). *Program Evaluation: Patterns and Directions.* (pp. 246–65) Washington D.C.: American Society for Public Administration.

2

Building Evaluation Capacity Within Organizations[1]

Richard C. Sonnichsen

The primary theme of this book is the institutionalization of evaluation. However, evaluation, even if not universally accepted or mandated by governments, can be implemented within organizations wishing to improve their performance and their decision-making process. Notwithstanding its checkered acceptance in some countries as an aid to governance, evaluation has been demonstrated to be a useful tool at the organizational level. This chapter examines the advantages, disadvantages, and implementation process of institutionalizing evaluation at the organization level. The focus is on evaluation capacity development when decisions on the scope, timing, funding, and methodology are under the authority of the organization. The organization is the anchor for evaluation activity, to use the terminology adopted by Mayne et al. in Chapter 1.

Two key questions need to be addressed when looking at the issue of evaluation institutionalization at the organization level: (1) Selecting evaluators. The principle issue is to determine whether to develop and use evaluators within the organization, or to make use of evaluation expertise bought-in from outside, or some combination of these. (2) Locating the evaluation function within the organization. Here, the concern is whether to locate the evaluation function at a corporate level or at the program manager level (see Mayne et al., chapter 1, for a discussion of this issue in a governmental context). The debate here is sometimes characterized as whether to focus on centralized or decentralized evaluation.

These two issues are linked to the supply and demand theme regarding evaluation institutionalization which is central to this book. How an organization selects evaluators and locates its evaluation function determines the interaction of supply and demand. Whether this interaction facilitates or hinders evaluation institutionalization at the level of the organization is considered in this chapter. Using internal and/or external evaluators is considered, as are centralized and decentralized options. This is followed by a look at how best to make use of internal evaluators at the organization level. Finally, some conclusions are drawn regarding the building of evaluation capacity within organizations.

Anchoring Evaluation at the Organizational Level Using Internal or External Evaluators

Discussions about the efficacy of internal vs. external evaluators oftentimes becomes polemic emphasizing the superiority of one approach over the other. This ill-focused argument fails to recognize that a more productive discussion would explore which approach is more appropriate to secure the needed information and present it to appropriate officials on a timely basis. The emphasis in this chapter is on examining the conditions which determine which approach is most appropriate. In the discussion that follows, internal evaluators are defined as those employed permanently by the organization and designated to conduct evaluations. External evaluators are those outside the organization, contracted on a periodic basis to perform evaluations selected by the organization.

Internal Evaluators

Using internal evaluators can not only be of assistance to the organization but may be the most appropriate first step in the development of the appreciation and benefits of the use of evaluation as a tool to assist in the broader governance process. Individual organizations that recognize the value of internal evaluators can initiate evaluation within their organizations without government mandates, but simply because it makes good management sense.

Internal evaluators can serve as a source of independent information to assist program managers and organization executives in the formulation, design, implementation, and eventual assessment of the impact of organization programs. This approach to managing organization activities can benefit the achievement of organization goals and objectives. By developing a close relationship between evaluators and program administrators, not only can the effectiveness of the program be determined , but the organization administrators can learn, from the evaluators, about the use and value of the tool of evaluation.

Another one of the advantages of internal evaluators is that evaluators can help organizations "learn." Argyris (1982) defines organizational learning as a "process of detecting and correcting error." The organizational learning process, as depicted by Argyris, is an iterative process of applying knowledge to solve recurring organizational problems. Evaluators can review programs and problem areas and develop data that help in the assimilation of knowledge by the organization. Independent evaluators have the ability to examine issues with an unbiased approach, thereby helping correct problem areas that have plagued organizations on a continuing basis. According to Rist (1994) government organizations appear to be more receptive to information produced internally than that which comes from external sources. He cites examples of this phenomenon in the United States and Canada and suggests that the credibility of internally produced material is greater if the recipients know that it has come from within their own organization.

The ultimate goal of internal evaluators is to have an influence on organizational decisions. By providing decision makers with independent, unbiased, empirical data, evaluators can improve the organizational decision-making process and organizational performance. For example, in 1974 the United States Federal Bureau of Investigation (FBI) internal evaluation staff was asked by the Director of the FBI to initiate a comprehensive review of the FBI's approach to investigative activities. This resulted in a five-year project that significantly reoriented the direction of investigative activities. The evaluation determined that the traditional measures of FBI performance, emphasizing quantitative statistical accomplishments, were misrepresenting the FBI's performance and directing resources to areas productive in accomplishment data, but of minimal value in accomplishing the FBI's mission of attacking complex criminal enterprises. The evaluation recommended a completely new approach to investigative activities emphasizing the quality or potential impact of a case instead of the quantity of cases being investigated. The recommendation was approved and resulted in successful investigations of criminal cartels in organized crime, illegal drugs, and public officials involved in corruption. The evaluators, in this instance, brought fresh insight and an independent review to the traditional approach to investigations.

Another example of the impact of internal evaluators was a 1986 study conducted in the United States Food and Drug Administration (FDA) of the FDA food sanitation inspection process. By manipulating the databases available to the program manager, an FDA evaluator discovered that food processing organizations found to be in violation of FDA regulations by FDA inspectors were more likely to be in violation during subsequent inspections, while firms with a clean bill of health tended to remain so. The evaluator recommended that food inspectors concentrate their limited resources on those firms in violation. No formal report was prepared in this instance but charts and graphs prepared by the evaluator were used to convince the program personnel of the advantages of altering their approach to food sanitation inspections. These examples show that internal evaluators can have an impact on their organizations if they take into consideration the organizational environment and structure the practice of evaluation to accommodate unique organizational characteristics.

Internal evaluators have a significantly different orientation from external evaluators employed on contract. They have a responsibility to act in the capacity of a consulting firm, diagnosing and correcting problems (Love, 1983). The internal evaluator challenges assumptions and values, creating alternatives in a supporting mode to the organizational decision-making process (Clifford and Sherman, 1983). Internal evaluators, by being employed by the organization, have a long-term commitment and can act in the capacity of change agents, increasing organizational performance (Sonnichsen, 1988). However, not every issue in an organization is a candidate for examination by internal evaluators. Organizations employing internal evaluators must examine each evaluation project and determine whether the use of internal or external evaluators is the best approach.

External Evaluators

Although internal evaluators can, over time develop a reputation for independence and objectivity, there may be a perception of bias or defensive posturing when internal evaluators furnish information on major policy debates to be used outside the organization. In these instances, it may be more appropriate to secure the services of outside consultants who bring a greater perception of independence to the public policy debate. External evaluators can be brought in by the organization when outside objectivity is thought to be necessary.

For some purposes, external evaluators appear to have an advantage over internal evaluators regarding objectivity since they perform the evaluation function from outside the organization on contract, and owe no allegiance or agreement to the organization, its mission or values. They simply conduct the prescribed evaluation and leave the report with the organization for further processing. Also, some policy issues demand the credibility that accrues to an outside view. If the findings need to be reported to a centralized parliamentary body, and credibility is an issue, then it may be more appropriate to use an external contractor.

Discussions concerning the advantages and disadvantages of internal versus external evaluators should focus not only on personnel and organizational issues, but also on the purpose of the evaluation efforts and how the findings are to be used. The audience and client for the evaluation are important considerations when determining if internal or external evaluators will be the most effective approach to producing useful information. In addition, external evaluators may be used because there are no evaluation skills within the organization, or no resources to staff a full-time internal evaluation function. In such circumstances, organizations may choose to contract evaluation expertise from outside, using consultancy firms, academics or the like.

If an organization chooses to use external evaluators on a full-time basis, it may still require a small internal staff to select issues for evaluation, administer and oversee the work of the external evaluators, monitor their performance, judge the quality of their work, review their invoices, and act as the linkage between the external evaluators and the management of the organization. It is important for internal evaluators reviewing the work of external evaluators to ensure that the evaluation represents an objective and independent assessment from their perspective and not a biased reinforcement of management's viewpoint.

External evaluators may also be the key to the successful implementation of an internal evaluation staff function in organizations. Without skilled personnel in an organization, with experience in evaluation procedures, it may be necessary to temporarily employ external evaluators to act as consultants and to train personnel chosen for the evaluation staff. External evaluators can be used during the formation of an internal evaluation staff and afterward to periodically assist and train evaluators or to provide advice and support, as the following two examples illustrate.

The U.S. Environmental Protection Agency Air Quality Office employed an evaluation consultant to help them establish a new evaluation office, write an evaluation handbook for the evaluators, and train new employees in evaluation techniques. The consultant remained available throughout the year to render advice and present training workshops.

The FBI evaluation staff annually contracts with an evaluation consultant to review the major evaluation reports published during the year. The consultant furnishes comments on the reports during annual evaluation training workshops and uses the material in the reports to create an educational dialog with the evaluation staff and illustrate good evaluation techniques. The external consultant is also available throughout the year for advice on specific evaluations.

Combining Internal and External Evaluators

Some evaluations may benefit from a combination of internal and external evaluators, combining the knowledge of the internal staff with the objectivity and fresh outlook of the external contractor. One hybrid approach is to establish an internal evaluation staff that periodically contracts out evaluations to evaluators when appropriate. This approach overcomes the independence issue, yet allows organizations to take advantage of their internal evaluator's familiarity with the culture and programs and their ability to respond quickly to the needs of decision makers. The internal evaluator then becomes the contact point for the external evaluator, assisting in the contracting process, selecting programs and issues for external evaluation, and assisting the external evaluators in cultural familiarization and organizational and political issues. This internal/external combination may be an optimum configuration for organizations attempting to build evaluation capacity since it combines the advantages of both approaches to evaluation, blending outside methodological skills and experience with the program and organizational culture knowledge of internal personnel.

A good example of linking internal and external evaluators is the experience of the National Science Foundation (NSF) in the United States. At the NSF evaluations originate and are managed from an internal evaluation office, yet the production of evaluation reports is contracted out to evaluation firms, partly because the internal office does not have a staff large enough to do evaluations internally (House, Haug, and Norris, 1996).

Other alternatives exist for combining some of the benefits of internal and external evaluators. In Ireland, in the early and mid 1990s, four evaluation units were established to monitor and review programs funded through European Union (EU) structural funds aid to Ireland. These four evaluation units are independent of the Irish national administration and conduct primarily summative evaluations with a "clear public accountability focus" (Boyle, 1997). Although in existence for only a brief time, there are indications that the evaluations produced are beginning to have some impact at both the policy and operational levels (ESF Programme Evaluation Unit, 1995). As mentioned, the evaluation units are independent of the national administration but with close links to their host departments, being housed in the same offices and managed by staff who have transferred from civil service departments. They do not have close ties to their programs but neither do they have the distance from the programs usually experienced by evaluators on contract. Boyle describes these evaluation units as neither internal nor external but a hybrid which he labels "independent."

A further related matter is the issue of when to use subject matter experts as evaluators. Do you need professionals who have both evaluation expertise and subject matter expertise? Do you use external consultants for subject matter or evaluation expertise? Subject matter experts may be required to assist evaluators in those instances where expertise is lacking on the evaluation staff and a particularly complex issue is under evaluation. Normally, evaluators can acquire sufficient program knowledge to conduct a comprehensive review. However, occasionally a difficult and vexing problem may require expertise beyond the skills and capabilities of the evaluation staff. When this dilemma is confronted, outside subject matter experts can be consulted or in some cases the appropriate expertise can be located within the organization in another department not affected by the evaluation. Universities are a good source of independent subject matter experts who can either temporarily join the evaluation team or act in a consultative capacity during the term of the evaluation.

Since all evaluation situations are unique, organizations should move away from dependency on a singular approach to evaluation and look at the appropriateness issue. Neither internal nor external evaluators are appropriate for all evaluation scenarios. It is critically important for evaluators and organization executives to review the evaluation question, the client, and the intended audience before committing to one approach or the other.

Anchoring Evaluation at the Organizational Level; Centralized and Decentralized Options

In addition to determining the merit of internal versus external evaluators, an additional debate revolves around the issue of locating evaluation at the program manager level or with a corporate group: opting for centralized or decentralized evaluation offices in organizations. The evaluation function in organizations can either be centralized at the headquarters of the organization or decentralized in various levels and locations throughout the organization.[2] No consensus has been formed on this issue and both types of arrangements as well as combinations can be found in government agencies. For organizations attempting to build an evaluation capacity, there are two primary issues to consider before deciding on a centralized or decentralized evaluation function.

First among the considerations to examine, when determining the proper location for the evaluation function, is the purpose of the evaluations. Although evaluations have many purposes, a dichotomous structuring of formative/developmental and summative/accountability conveniently captures the focus of many approaches to evaluation (Boyle, 1993). The delineating criteria to examine before choosing one of these two approaches are the intended uses and audiences for the evaluation information, and the necessity for the perception of independence. If the primary focus of evaluation activity is accountability, performance assessment, or production of data for use in public policy debates, then a centralized approach, utilizing a corporate evaluation group, may be the most appropriate. If, on the other hand, the purpose of the evaluation is organizational improvement and building a sustainable capacity to assist program managers achieve their goals, a decentralized option, locating evaluation at the program level, may be more appropriate.

Second, legislative requirements and established government rules for the production of information, ministerial regulations, and organizational authority levels for program development and implementation, need to be examined before deciding on a centralized or decentralized evaluation function. As previously discussed, for an evaluation function to be effective, evaluators have to be independent and have unrestricted access to data and personnel. If any of this is proscribed by rules and regulations, these constraints need to be considered when determining where the evaluation function will be located. The specific advantages and disadvantages of centralized and decentralized evaluation are discussed below.

Centralized Evaluation

Centralized evaluation offices have the advantage of being able to develop a skilled cadre of evaluators who are able to work independently with minimal bias since they have no attachment to any particular organization program. The combination of evaluation skills and independence enhances centralized evaluation credibility, and over time a centralized evaluation staff will develop an institutional memory that benefits the organization. Centralizing the location of the evaluation staff also benefits the organization by allowing the systematic development of a strategic evaluation plan for reviewing organization programs. Results and findings issued by centralized evaluation offices are more widely disseminated and more likely to be reviewed and debated.

A centralized model of evaluation was established in Canada in 1978 (McQueen, 1992). The Office of Controller General (OCG) was created as the central agency to oversee evaluation units set up in each agency of government. The OCG set goals and procedures for the evaluation units who report to the deputy minister in each agency. Evaluations are expected to address relevant and significant questions, yield credible findings and recommendations, and be cost-justified (Segsworth, 1990). The deputy ministers play an important role during the evaluations and the heads of the ministries are the clients for the evaluations. Reviews of the evaluation function in Canada by the OCG has revealed that both instrumental and conceptual use of evaluations has occurred and a significant number of the evaluations led to a reallocation of resources (Mayne, 1994).

The primary downside to centralized units is the threatening nature of their evaluative activities as perceived by other organizational components. Centralized evaluation reports receive scrutiny at upper levels of management in the organization and identified program deficiencies may be the subject of recommendations to alter program operations. It is common for evaluation units to identify areas in programs that need improvement and recommend changes. Since change creates uncertainty, and uncertainty creates resistance to change, the relationship between centralized evaluation units and program personnel is likely to be strained, particularly if recommended changes are not mutually agree upon. It is difficult if not impossible to separate the leadership of a program from the program itself during an evaluation. This places a burden on the program manager during a centralized evaluation that may not be present if the evaluation is conducted by evaluators assigned to an evaluation office attached to the program or at least at a level closer to the program.

There may be a tendency for centralized evaluation units in large organizations to develop the "ideology" of the incumbent administration which diminishes their independence and introduces the possibility of bias (Chelimsky, 1985). Chelimsky also reports that in the United States the high turnover in political appointees requires centralized evaluation units to conduct shorter studies to ensure survival and not the longer term effectiveness studies which is one of the purported major benefits of centralized evaluation units.

Decentralized Evaluation

Decentralized evaluation units are located close to the programs they serve with the primary purpose to support the decision-making process and improve program effectiveness and efficiency. Decentralized evaluation staffs reduce the threat level to program managers during evaluations since the evaluators are close to the program, have a greater familiarity with the program operation, and circulate their reports at lower levels in the organization. However, this closeness to the program presents one of the major drawbacks to decentralized evaluation units, the potential for bias, due to familiarity with the program and program personnel. The issue of independence of decentralized units, arising from their closeness to the program and program personnel, tends to erode the credibility of their findings and lessens the impact of the evaluation as viewed by senior management and external interests. The potential for bias and the failure to inform the top levels of the organization of evaluation findings combine to diminish the effectiveness of this approach to evaluation as viewed from a macro organizational perspective. However, as previously noted, this may be the appropriate approach for organizations wishing to monitor the implementation of programs.

Another tension for decentralized evaluation occurs when evaluation practice is decentralized, but program decision-making regarding resource use and allocation remains largely centralized. In Britain, local Training and Enterprise Councils (TECs) were set up to develop workforce skills and help to improve training. A largely decentralized evaluation strategy was pursued whereby TECs were required to evaluate themselves. Their corporate and business plans must contain an evaluation strategy and an account of the evaluation work to be undertaken in the coming year (Marquand, 1992). Yet information emerging from local evaluations, while useful, was not deemed sufficient at central government department level to facilitate measurement of differential costs and examine the reasons for these. Consequently, a national system of standardized performance indicators has been introduced, following extensive dialogue with TECs, to facilitate central decision-making, and complement decentralized evaluation practice (Morrey, 1995).

Another option to consider is the combination of centralized and decentralized units. Depending on the size of the organization and the autonomy of departments, this arrangement may function either with a cooperative arrangement among the units or with independent evaluation units. Decentralized evaluation units may function independently or they may share findings with the centralized evaluation staff. Centralized evaluation units may set evaluation agendas for the entire organization with decentralized units actually conducting the evaluation. Or there may be minimal communication between centralized and decentralized units, each functioning separately and reporting findings to the senior management staff of their respective environments.

Both centralized and decentralized approaches to evaluation have their merits with the choice largely being which approach is more appropriate for an organization. A significant question to be answered by senior managers is the goal evaluation is expected to achieve. Effectiveness evaluations are more credible if conducted by a competent centralized evaluation unit away from the program. If external entities are expected to review the evaluation results, then the credibility that flows from centralized, independent, assessment may be more appropriate. A good example is evaluation in the United States National Science Foundation, cited earlier. House, Haug, and Norris (1996) indicate that demand for NSF evaluation data is strongly driven by Congress, and focuses on impacts. A central evaluation office was seen as the best means for the NSF to facilitate this demand. On the other hand, decentralized evaluation units may be better equipped to review implementation problems and offer solutions to problems due to their comprehensive understanding of the program and its environment.

Decentralized evaluation structures may also facilitate participatory and empowerment evaluation practices. Centralized evaluation studies with a prime accountability focus may be viewed by front-line or field level staff and managers as a threat, used to control their activities rather than stimulate performance (Bamberger, 1989). Participatory evaluation, on the other hand, facilitated by decentralizing evaluation to the field level, aims to empower people and facilitate learning and development at the local level (Naryan, 1993).

Since public policy issues are complex and subject to shifting priorities and conditions, the evaluation function should also be capable of a

---

Box 2.1: Advantages and Disadvantages of Evaluation Options

	ADVANTAGES	DISADVANTAGES
INTERNAL EVALUATORS	Familiarity with organization. Facilitates program improvement. Credibility. Develops institutional memory. Monitor and follow up recommendations.	Lack of independence. Perceived organizational bias. Ethical dilemmas. Burden of additional tasks. Possible lack of power.
EXTERNAL EVALUATORS	Superior skills. New perspectives. Independence and objectivity. Readily available skills. Facilitates program accountability.	Lack knowledge of organization. Limited access to information and people. Expensive Lack of follow up.
CENTRALIZED UNITS	Develops degree of independence. Develops institutional memory. Develops superior skills. Facilitates program accountability. Enables strategic planning of evaluations.	May appear threatening. Can be perceived as tool of agency. Remoteness from front line.
DECENTRALIZED UNITS	Greater program knowledge. Less resistance from managers. Facilitates participatory evaluations. Facilitates program improvement.	May lack independence. May lack methodological skills. Possible lack of power.

---

flexible response to changing environmental conditions. There should be no slavish adherence to any one particular approach to evaluation but rather a continuous determination of what approach is the most appropriate for a given situation. Box 2.1 summarizes some of the advantages and disadvantages of the internal, external, centralized, and decentralized options for evaluation.

Building an evaluation capacity within organizations is not straightforward and linear. Evaluation, by its nature, implies accountability and carries an implicit examination of the stewardship of programs. The paradox of evaluation is that many people see little to be gained from establishing an evaluation function, yet the use of information gained through independent assessment can be a valuable asset in making informed decisions about organization policies and program implementation. Recognizing the implicit threat and the probable resistance to evaluation, a strategy for implementing the evaluation function is imperative if evaluation is to have an impact on the organization.

Building Evaluation Expertise within Organizations

The discussion so far has concentrated on the internal/external evaluator and centralized/decentralized options for evaluation. However, whatever combination is chosen most organizations that are serious about building evaluation capacity will need to develop some level of evaluation expertise within the organization. Creating evaluation capacity within an organization by developing staff in the organization with evaluation skills requires more of the organization than does buying-in evaluation skills from outside for specific contracts. Consequently, this section explores the issues which need to be addressed to build evaluation expertise within the organization as a means to institutionalize evaluation.

It is crucial, when starting to implement an evaluation effort in an organization to choose issues to evaluate that are (1) relevant and (2) simple to understand by interested stakeholders. Choosing complex issues to evaluate requires lengthy evaluations causing people to lose interest in the outcome. Additionally, the understanding of the complexity of the elements involved will make it difficult to gain consensus and implement any recommendations. Beginning with a simple issue that will serve the decision makers needs will enhance the probability that evaluation can be implemented on a routine basis. The World Bank Operations Evaluation Department (OED) (1994) suggests starting evaluation implementation modestly with simple mechanisms that can be implemented immediately. Evaluation capacity can be built incrementally by being sensitive to the needs of the program personnel and an orientation to be helpful to them.

One of the more appropriate situations in which to introduce evaluation is during the implementation phase in the policy cycle (see Rist in chapter 5). This is particularly true of organizations responsible for interpreting program intent and choosing the appropriate approach to effective implementation. As Rist points out in chapter 5, evaluation can examine the translation of policy intent into operational efforts, reviewing resource usage, capacity for successful implementation, and the logic of the program vis a vis the problem it was designed to combat.

Participatory evaluation, using program personnel to assist full time evaluators, will help ensure ownership of the findings and increase the potential for the ultimate use of the evaluation information. Sensitivity to the governmental environment and organizational culture will enhance the credibility of the evaluators. The end product of evaluation should be focused on the need of the managers and decision makers and be shown to be a value added process worthy of the resources devoted to it.

One modest approach to the evaluation process may begin with identifying performance indicators, in conjunction with program personnel, and initiating the process of measuring and monitoring program activities. Use of this program data to improve the efficiency and impact of the program may contribute to lessening the tension generally generated by the conduct of an evaluation. Selection of evaluators from the ranks of employees with credibility among their peers is another approach that will help introduce the concept of evaluation in an organization. The use of a methodology that is acceptable to the culture of the client and audience for the evaluation will aid in the acceptance and use of evaluation findings. In many countries the use of a qualitative approach to data collection maybe more appropriate than a quantitative approach. Many developing countries do not share the Western fascination with numerical precision (Cuthbert, 1985).

Wide distribution of the evaluation findings with accompanying recommendations for change will help develop the sense of an evaluation ethic and demonstrate the value of internal evaluation process. Constructive use of the findings, in lieu of judging performance, will benefit the long range sustainability of evaluation as an integral part of the administrative apparatus of an organization. Failure to begin the building of evaluation capacity on a positive note, highlighting the positive aspects of the process, may well doom the evaluation function to oblivion.

By focusing on the needs of clients and engaging their program personnel in a constructive dialogue about program strengths and weaknesses, the evaluation function can be seen to be of assistance. Conflicts between evaluators and program personnel can be minimized through recognition by evaluators of the importance of clients and their needs.

The discussion in this chapter indicates that there are numerous conditions which affect the institutionalization of evaluation within organizations. The probability of success when establishing an evaluation function is increased when the following factors are considered.

Independence. The single most important factor to consider when establishing an evaluation function at any level in an organization is the granting of autonomy to the evaluation staff so that the data collected, the findings determined, and the recommendations presented are perceived as credible by organizational constituencies. Without this independence and freedom to access data and personnel, the evaluation function will be perceived as biased, and ignored. The independence of an evaluation staff is important since reported findings are subjected to intense scrutiny by interested stakeholders and if the results are perceived to be biased, their utility in public policy debates is severe eroded. The independence of an evaluation staff can be established by the head of a government agency, the chief executive officer of a private corporation, or a legislative body. For example, in the United States Federal Bureau of Investigation (FBI), the evaluation staff operates independently with access to all personnel and files. This authority was granted by the FBI Director and the evaluation staff reports to him directly through one of his Assistant Directors. Another illustration is provided by the Inspectors General Act of 1978, which established by law in the United States an internal review group in each of the executive branches of government that is required to report its findings independently to both the head of the agency and the U.S. Congress.

Availability of skilled evaluators. Although persons with social science research backgrounds and experience are the most desirable candidates for an evaluation staff, the absence of these skills does not preclude the development of an evaluation staff. Recruiting career organizational employees, with a knowledge of organization culture, programs, and history, can offset some of the benefits of using skilled social scientists. An evaluation staff can be developed using personnel from within the organization, directed by one or more social scientists. Consultants can be brought in to train and act as advisors during the formative development stages of an evaluation office. Universities can be a productive source of personnel with skills to assist in the development of an evaluation staff. The selection, development, and training of personnel for use as evaluators is discussed in more detail by Boyle in chapter 6.

Staffing. An evaluation office does not have to be large. Three to six evaluators are sufficient to begin an evaluation function in an organization. Several acceptable alternatives are available for selection of members of an evaluation staff. Optimally, as mentioned above, they would all be social scientists with experience in the organization. However, this is seldom the case and compromises have to be made. First, a determination needs to be made whether or not the evaluators will be assigned to the staff on a permanent basis or temporarily detailed to the staff for a predetermined amount of time. The advantage to a permanent staff is the ability of evaluators to develop an institutional memory and increase their skills and abilities with training. On the other hand, organization personnel selected to perform as evaluators for one to three or more years bring program knowledge and fresh views and ideas to the evaluation staff. An advantage to this latter scenario is that rotating evaluators exposes more persons in the organization to the benefits of evaluation. Over time this process helps integrate and develop an appreciation for evaluation in the organization. A mixture of permanent and temporarily assigned evaluators may be an optimum configuration, combining the benefits of both scenarios. Box 2.2 provides three examples of staffing alternatives for an evaluation office.

Authority Needed to Access Data and Personnel. One of the important considerations to examine before establishing an evaluation staff is the availability of data and access to personnel for evaluators. Without comprehensive and unrestricted access to program material and personnel, any resulting findings will be suspect. Data quality is also an important consideration. If data is unavailable or unreliable, then evaluators may be required to create original data bases for their evaluations. This is a time consuming effort and requires methodological skills that may not be available internally in the organization.

Location in the Organization. There are strong grounds for arguing that an evaluation office should be located where it reports to the head of the organization. By locating the evaluation office in this manner, and providing the director of the office with sufficient rank to be considered one of the organization executives, the evaluation office will be viewed as sufficiently independent from the organization programs to minimize the perception of bias when programs are reviewed. For example, at both the U.S. Food and Drug Administration and the FBI, the evaluation office is directed by a senior official who reports directly to the head of the agency. Both of these evaluation directors hold executive positions in their respective organizations. By locating these

---

Box 2.2: Staffing an Evaluation Office

During a 1990 survey of federal government evaluation offices in the United States, three different alternative methods for staffing these offices were encountered (Sonnichsen, 1991).

(1) The Federal Bureau of Investigation (FBI) selected potential evaluators from special agents with investigative experience who were interested in administrative advancement in the FBI and were willing to relocate to Washington, D.C. for a minimum of three to five years. These agents were trained in evaluation techniques and served for three to five years before being promoted to other positions in the FBI. Their investigative experience provided them with excellent training for evaluation and they were taught the necessary evaluation skills.

(2) The United States Bureau of Land Management (BLM) maintained a permanent staff of six experienced evaluators at their headquarters in Washington, D.C. who travelled around the United States training BLM field personnel in evaluation skills. These trained personnel were periodically placed together in teams of four to five for travel to other field offices to conduct evaluations. Upon completion of an evaluation, they returned to their own field offices resuming their regular duties until called upon to conduct another evaluation. Since the BLM evaluations are conducted primarily by non-evaluators, the BLM has prepared a detailed evaluation handbook for their use, with detailed descriptions of the steps and procedures to be used to conduct evaluations and explicit instructions on all facets of evaluation.

(3) The United States Food and Drug Administration (FDA) uses permanent evaluators that are selected for their analytical skills and educational backgrounds. They are hired both from within FDA and from outside the organization. They remain on the evaluation staff permanently, building an institutional memory and developing their analytical skills and knowledge of the FDA culture and programs.

---

evaluation offices at the executive level in the organization the independence of the evaluators is enhanced and the evaluation function becomes highly visible in the organization.

Evaluation Agenda. In order to be effective, evaluators need to develop an agreement with the head of the organization regarding the scope of their work, their authority to initiate evaluations, reporting requirements, and their relationship with both superiors and the program managers and personnel. For an evaluation staff to be successful, evaluators need to publicize their evaluation procedures within the organization so their activities and purpose are known and understood throughout the organization. This public image will aid in reducing the perceived threat and uncertainty that surrounds the evaluation function.

Credibility. The credibility of an evaluation staff is the most important characteristic that contributes to the success of evaluation. An evaluation staff that is viewed as credible and objective will facilitate the acceptance of findings and recommendations. The choice between internal and external evaluators essentially revolves around this central issue of objectivity. Which approach to evaluation is more objective and independent and therefore, by inference, better equipped to produce unbiased evaluation findings and reports?

Internal evaluators are unable to escape the obvious fact that they are employees of their organization and presumed to possess some allegiance to the organization and its basic mission and values. It is highly unlikely that evaluators, working for a company or government agency, do not share, at a minimum, the core values of the organization. Nevertheless, this allegiance should not impede evaluators from examining other than core issues and properly conducting high quality, objective evaluations.

The key to independence and credibility is agreement between evaluators and the hierarchy of the organization that evaluators will be free to evaluate organization programs without interference from executive management, and that the findings and recommendations will be published and debated over their potential impact on the organization.

Conclusion

Critical to the building of an evaluation capacity in organizations is an awareness of both the benefits and potential pitfalls of the use of program evaluation as a tool to assist in the development of organizations. The experiences of organizations in countries where evaluation capacity has already been developed and the lessons they have learned can be profitably used by organizations experimenting with evaluation, thereby helping avoid some of the impediments encountered to institutionalization of evaluation at the organization level.

In an era of rapid social change and economic uncertainty, program evaluation should be an integral element in the administration of organizations with evaluators reviewing organizational programs independently and developing empirical evidence of their relevance, success, and cost-effectiveness. Evaluation in organizations can contribute to the public policy process by acting as a conduit for program performance information from the program implementation level to organizational decision makers responsible for setting policy direction. Evaluators also assist organizations by supplying information to meet the organizational demand. It is important to recognize the proper balance between the needs of the organizations for information and the capability of the evaluation staff to provide it.

This chapter has shown that some demands are better met by internal evaluators than external, and vice versa. Similarly, centralized and decentralized evaluation units meet differing demands. In particular, it would seem that where program improvement is the main goal, with the focus mainly on operational issues, using internal evaluators based at the program management level may be the most appropriate response. Alternatively, where the main focus is on program impacts and accountability, external evaluators or centralized corporate evaluation units within organizations have particular strengths. The main danger is of a possible mismatch of supply and demand. Evaluation units staffed by insiders and located at the program management level are unlikely to take root in an organization if they are being asked to undertake effectiveness studies for accountability purposes.

Organization-based evaluation is a constructive activity designed to develop information about how programs work. Internal evaluators have the advantages of institutional memory, knowledge of organizational operations, identification with and understanding of organizational culture, ability for follow-up, and credibility within the organization. The downside for internal evaluators is the potential to develop a myopia that masks a bias, thereby diminishing the quality of the evaluation and its value to management as a decision-making tool. External evaluators, on the other hand, possess objectivity and independence, but may not completely understand organizational culture and program operations. Additionally, because of their outside status, they lack the ability to conduct follow-up on recommendations. Unfamiliarity with organizational culture, personalities and operations may preclude in-depth examination of programs.

Centralized evaluation units have their independence, skill level, and institutional memory function to recommend them, yet they also possess the potential to become political tools of the organizational hierarchy if they are not explicitly granted their independence. Decentralized evaluation staffs, on the other hand, may be insulated from the politics of the agency administration, yet may succumb to bias due to their closeness to the program managers and program personnel.

Organizations attempting the institutionalization of the evaluation function may profitably begin with the use of both internal and external evaluators. Particularly during the implementation stage of evaluation there are advantages to using the skills and experience of external evaluators along with the organizational knowledge of the internal evaluators. The choice of placing the evaluation function in a centralized or decentralized location in the organization depends, to a great extent, on the purpose and intended use of the evaluation information and the structure of the organization. Both variations have merit and can function cooperatively together.

The keys to successful location of the evaluation function in an organization are comprehensive examination of the organizational culture, the organizational requirements for information, and available resources, coupled with a well developed strategic evaluation plan setting forth the purpose and goals of evaluation. Initiation of the evaluation function in an organization is not an overnight occurrence but a methodical implementation process demonstrating the value of this technique to support organizational decision-making and assist in solving organizational problems. It will be necessary during the early stages of initiating evaluation in an organization to continually market the efficacy of this process as a beneficial activity for the organization. Sustaining an evaluation function in an organization requires an explicit recognition of the value added by evaluation to accomplishing organizational goals.

Notes

1. While reference is made to organizations, this discussion covers anchoring evaluation at the program level, as well as at the corporate level within individual organizations.
2. Decentralized evaluation units referred to in this chapter are those located at the program level within the organization.

References

Argyris, C. 1982. *Reasoning, Learning, and Action.* San Francisco: Jossey-Bass Publishers.

Bamberger, M. 1989. "The Monitoring and Evaluation of Public Sector Programs in Asia: Why are Development Programs Monitored but not Evaluated?" *Evaluation Review*, 13, 3:223–43.

Boyle, R. 1993. *Making Evaluation Relevant: A Study of Policy and Programme Evaluation Practice in the Irish Public Sector.* Dublin, Ireland: Institute of Public Administration.

Boyle, R. 1997. *Evaluating Public Expenditure Programmes: Determining a Role for Programme Review.* Committee for Public Management Research Discussion Paper No. 1. Dublin, Ireland: Institute of Public Administration.

Chelimsky, E. 1985. "Old Patterns and New Directions in Program Evaluation". In E. Chelimsky (ed.), *Program Evaluation: Patterns and Directions* (pp. 1–35). Washington, D.C.: The American Society for Public Administration.

Clifford, D.L. and Sherman, P. 1983. "Internal Evaluation: Integrating Program Evaluation and Management". In A.J. Love (ed.), *Developing Effective Internal Evaluation. New Directions for Program Evaluation* (pp.23–45) San Francisco: Jossey-Bass.

Cuthbert, M. 1985. "Evaluation Encounters in Third World Settings: A Caribbean Perspective." In M.Q. Patton (ed.) *Culture and Evaluation. New Directions for Program Evaluation* (pp.29–36) San Francisco: Jossey-Bass.

ESF Programme Evaluation Unit. 1995. *Impact of Evaluations.* Department of Enterprise and Employment, Dublin, Ireland: ESF Programme Evaluation Unit.

House, E.R., Haug, C., and Norris, N. 1996. "Producing Evaluations in a Large Bureaucracy." *Evaluation*, 2, 2: 135–50.

Love, A. J. 1983. "The Organizational Context and the Development of Internal Evaluation." In A J. Love (ed.), *Developing Effective Internal Evaluation. New Directions For Program Evaluation* (pp.5–22). San Francisco: Jossey Bass.

Marquand, J. 1992. "Evaluation, Decentralization and Accountability". *Policy Studies*, 13, 1:30–39.

Mayne, J. 1994. "Utilizing Evaluation in Organizations: The Balancing Act." In F. Leeuw, R. Rist, and R. Sonnichsen (eds.), *Can Governments Learn? Comparative Perspectives on Evaluation & Organizational Learning.* New Brunswick, N. J.: Transaction Publishers.

McQueen, C. 1992. "Program Evaluation in the Canadian Federal Government." In J. Hudson, J. Mayne, and R. Thomlison (eds.), *Action-Oriented Evaluation in Organizations: Canadian Practices* (pp.28–47)Toronto, Ontario: Wall & Emerson, Inc.

Morrey, L. 1995. Characteristics of Performance Indicators: Lessons from Department of Employment. Unpublished paper presented at performance management seminar, London.

Naryan, D. 1993. Participatory Evaluation: Tools for Managing Change in Water and Sanitation. World Bank Technical Paper No. 207. Washington, DC: The World Bank.

Rist, R. 1994. "The Preconditions for Learning: Lessons From the Public Sector." In F. Leeuw, R. Rist, and R. Sonnichsen (eds.), *Can Governments Learn: Comparative Perspectives on Evaluation and Organizational Learning.* New Brunswick, N. J. : Transaction Books.

Segsworth, R. V. 1990. "Policy and Program Evaluation in the Government of Canada." In R. C. Rist (ed.), *Program Evaluation and the Management of Government: Patterns & Prospects across Eight Nations* (pp.21–36), New Brunswick: Transaction Publishers.

Sonnichsen, R. C. 1988. "Advocacy Evaluation: A Model for Internal Evaluation Offices." *Evaluation and Program Planning*, 11(2), 141–48.

Sonnichsen, R.C. 1991. *Characteristics of High Impact Internal Evaluation Offices.* DPA diss., University of Southern California.

The World Bank. 1994. Building Evaluation Capacity. In *Lessons and Practices*, Operations Evaluation Department.

3

Evaluation Coverage

Yoon-Shik Lee

There has been little in-depth discussion, in theory or in practice, of what should be covered in evaluation, although there have been quite a few studies on how to evaluate (see Chelimsky, 1985; Rowe, 1983). In this regard, this chapter aims to elaborate on evaluation coverage in the context of evaluation capacity development.

To that end, the following questions are worth addressing: First, why is it so important for the development of evaluation capacity to practically define evaluation coverage? Second, in relation to evaluation capacity development, why is evaluation coverage important? Third, how much and in what way should an evaluation be done? Fourth, what type of evaluation should be done? Fifth, what are, if any, the constraints on the institutionalization of assessment in terms of evaluation coverage?

This chapter attempts to suggest what good practice is in terms of evaluation coverage. Due to the lack of empirical data on evaluation coverage, discussion is based solely upon the cases of several particular countries, with the analyses derived through inductive reasoning. Therefore, a certain amount of caution is required in interpretation, so as not to make an over-generalization.

What Evaluation Coverage Means

Generally, the term "coverage" has been understood in the context of program coverage, which is the target of process evaluation (e.g., monitoring). However, one does not often talk about the term "evaluation coverage." There tends to be some misunderstandings about the terminology, and it is thus necessary to define the concept of evaluation coverage. I will first clarify what it means in this study, lest the following discussion on the subject mislead readers.

"Evaluation coverage" in the public sector refers to (i) the extent or comprehensiveness of coverage of government activities; (ii) the degree to which evaluation is done on a targeted object in an evaluation system; and (iii) the assessment of different types of government-related activities. As such, evaluation coverage is not limited to programs and/or policies. Rather, it covers whatsoever is required, mandated, or authorized to be evaluated by the government authorities concerned including government departments, executive agencies, or audit offices.

As already pointed out above, evaluation coverage should not be confused with program coverage, which mainly focuses on the procedural issues about program implementation such as how and to what extent activities have been implemented as intended; whether they are targeted to appropriate populations or problems; and to what extent the target population is covered (i.e., delivered goods and services) by a program (for a detailed discussion on program coverage, see Rossi and Freeman, 1993). In the context of program coverage, targeting has to do with both the objects (i.e., problems or populations) at which a program's activities are directed and the coverage that these activities achieve. With regard to evaluation coverage, targeting has to do with the objects (e.g., activities or organizations) for which an evaluation is to be done. Thus, even though the term "coverage" is commonly used in the two types of evaluation, the meaning each terminology suggests is quite different. Program coverage in process evaluation indicates the extent to which a program serves the intended target population, whereas evaluation coverage in any type of assessment suggests not only the degree to which an activity or entity was evaluated but also the extent of what was actually evaluated regardless of the type of the object.

Why Evaluation Coverage is Important

There are several reasons why we should clarify evaluation coverage. First, decisions on evaluation coverage determine what the government agencies and departments responsible for evaluation are actually supposed to do. Second decisions on evaluation coverage determine the foci of evaluation. In this regard, focal points of an evaluation may include economic efficiency, effectiveness, implementation process, organization performance, and so forth. Thus, to decide on evaluation coverage is important in the sense that it is likely to affect the direction of an evaluation. Third, evaluation coverage affects decisions on the type of evaluation methods or techniques. Technically speaking, evaluation methods depend on evaluation approaches such as front-end analysis, process evaluation and effectiveness evaluation. Evaluation approaches are decided on the basis of what an evaluation needs to cover (Smith, 1981). In other words, it is logical that the objects of an evaluation determine what types of approaches are required for an evaluation, which in turn decides what kinds of methods or techniques are needed for the evaluation. In all, what is to be covered in evaluation makes a great impact on what type of evaluation approaches, including evaluation methods or techniques, are used.

The Comprehensiveness of Evaluation Coverage

In an effort to institutionalize evaluation and build evaluation capacity, a critical issue is what types of government activity should be evaluated. In other words, how comprehensive should evaluation coverage be? This is not an easy problem to tackle. The comprehensiveness of evaluation coverage tends to vary not only with country but also with evaluation systems within a country. Furthermore, objective criteria do not exist for assessing the comprehensiveness of evaluation coverage. Under the circumstances, though not the best, it appears to be desirable to take a closer look at the cases of countries which have already experienced evaluation coverage. An examination of these countries' cases may help uncover some interesting facts regarding the comprehensiveness of evaluation coverage, though this can be but a partial understanding.

Governments and administrators across the nations vary significantly in their approaches to encouraging the comprehensiveness of evaluation coverage. In the United Kingdom and New Zealand, for example, evaluation is essentially dispersed and fragmentary in nature. In the United Kingdom, as Pollitt (1993) notes, "policy evaluation has never found a secure or permanent home near the heart of a (relatively centralized) state machine." There is little central coordination or control of policy and program evaluation. This is at least in part due to the general policy of devolution of responsibility to individual departments and agencies, including responsibility for evaluating their activities. In New Zealand, responsibility for evaluation is dispersed too. The scale of evaluation work is small. Some government departments undertake their own evaluation activities, and a small number have operational units dedicated to that purpose. However, program evaluation is not a commonplace or widespread activity (Olson, 1996). Similarly, the focus of evaluation in Germany is on the departmental level of government. Central political and administrative institutions do not play an active role.

By way of contrast the federal governments in Australia and Canada have encouraged a coherent approach to evaluation across the public service. In Australia, the government's strategy for evaluation requires annual planning for systematic and comprehensive monitoring of the efficiency and effectiveness of existing programs. Each program is expected to have some major evaluation coverage over a three- to five year cycle. Departments must outline the extent of their evaluation activities in Portfolio Evaluation Plans. (Commonwealth of Australia 1991: 1–26; Australian Audit Office 1992: 2–6).

In Canada, all departments and agencies at the federal level are required to develop evaluation policies which are compatible with Treasury Board policy. This departmental policy outlines the organizational aspects, roles, responsibilities and accountability of officers involved. It describes procedures for carrying out evaluations and for decision-making based on findings. Departmental policy establishes the framework within which evaluation planning takes place. There are two interrelated plans. The first is a long-term evaluation strategy that contains two elements—a program evaluation profile and a program evaluation schedule. The second is an annual plan of evaluation activities proposed for the upcoming fiscal year. In terms of coverage, the government-wide Program Review procedure indicated in the 1995 Budget that all federal programs should be reviewed to ensure the most effective and cost-efficient way of delivering programs and services. The Review policy does not require departments to review all of their programs and policies over a prescribed period of time. Rather, the emphasis is put on identifying priorities e.g. programs that are essential to meet the government's broad goals; programs that are subject to greater risk in terms of implementation delivery or cost (Annual Report to Parliament by the President of the Treasury Board 1995:12).

Other governments and countries fall between these two scenarios in terms of the comprehensiveness of coverage. Ireland provides an interesting example of a mix of comprehensive coverage for a specific sector of activity, and sporadic coverage elsewhere. The comprehensive evaluation coverage is for programs and projects funded through the European Union Structural Funds, designed to help member states overcome problems of a structural nature that slow down or inhibit the economic development of certain regions, enterprises and individuals. Under European Union regulations, the Structural Funds must be evaluated within a framework of partnership between the European Commission and the member state. In Ireland, prior appraisal, monitoring, interim assessment and ex-post evaluation of the funds are carried out for all of the programs operated under the Structural Funds. For other sectors of government activity, however, evaluation coverage is more sporadic, following the dispersed approach to evaluation found in the United Kingdom and New Zealand. However, with the introduction of three-yearly program reviews in 1997, Ireland is moving to comprehensive evaluation coverage of government expenditure programs (Boyle, 1997).

In terms of institutionalizing evaluation coverage, it would seem that the devolved approach, with governments encouraging departments and agencies to evaluate, but not providing central coordination and direction, is not fully effective. Individual evaluations may well be carried out in exemplary fashion. That is, some departments or agencies develop good coverage. Comprehensive coverage however does not seem to happen in this approach because there is no central mechanism for coordinating overall evaluations of government activities (e.g., programs or policies). The Canadian and Australian approach provides a more appropriate mechanism for encouraging comprehensive evaluation coverage of government programs and policies. Here, there is a strong emphasis on systematically integrating evaluation into corporate and program management and planning, with a requirement that each program have some major evaluation coverage over a three- to five-year cycle. Planning for evaluation is a required activity. There is also strong central coordination and encouragement of evaluation coverage: the Department of Finance in Australia and the Office of the Comptroller and Auditor General in Canada both provide guidance, encouragement, and quality control, rather than prescription and detailed interference.

This does not mean that comprehensive coverage of programs is easy or always fully possible. Box 3.1 provides an illustration of Australian experience with their first round of comprehensive program evaluation coverage. Their experience, like that of Canada who has a longer history in attempting comprehensive coverage, is that it is too ambitious to expect full coverage of programs every three to five years. Priorities must be set, and limitations in the process be acknowledged.

In Canada, for example, coverage is assessed from a number of perspectives (Annual Report to Parliament by the President of the Treasury Board 1995: 12–15):

* *Government priorities.* The government has set central review priorities, especially those that cut across departments or cover larger blocks of programming.
* *Major programming.* Since 1991/92 departments have reviewed about 74 to 84 percent of major expenditure programs in a "significant" way. Significant here is taken to mean that most of the elements of the activity have been covered for several aspects of performance: rationale, success, compliance or cost effectiveness.
* *Reviews by type of government function.* Since 1992, virtually all federal regulations have been reviewed.
* *Administrative policy.* The Treasury Board Manual contains twenty-three different administrative policy areas, of which nineteen might be expected to be reviewed in departments, chiefly by audits. Since 1991–92, all policy areas have been addressed by at least some departments, and nine were examined by most.
* *Performance Measurement Systems.* A study found that 60 percent of the systems examined did not address impacts. It also found that there has been limited integration of performance measures with management practices. At the same time, some examples of excellent efforts were noted.

Multiple Perspectives and the Implications for the Extent of Coverage

Many institutions and individuals can get involved in the evaluation process, resulting in the development of evaluation coverage from a number of different perspectives. In Canada, for example, the Office of the Comptroller and Auditor General, the deputy heads of departments and agencies, evaluation units within departments, Treasury Board, Cabinet Policy Committees, and the Auditor General, all have important roles to play in the evaluation process and influence the degree of evaluation coverage of targeted objects. Mayne, Divorski, and Lemaire discuss this issue of multiple locations and their implications for evaluation coverage in some detail in chapter 1.

There are thus a range of stakeholders involved in conducting evaluations. In many situations, the "official" goals or objectives of the program or policy under scrutiny tend to form the basis for the evaluation, as the funders and policy officials have the highest power in the evaluation process and tend to judge programs and policies against formal goals and objectives. This position has come under criticism for ignor-

---

Box 3.1: Evaluation Coverage in the Australian Public Service

An evaluation strategy was implemented as part of program management and budgeting in 1987. The expectation was that most programs would be subject to some form of major program evaluation activity at least once every three to five years.

An evaluation of progress made in 1992 found that this expectation may have been too ambitious, given that many of the agencies had only limited experience and knowledge of the resource implications. Further, agencies pragmatically interpreted "comprehensive coverage" as requiring them to conduct at least one major evaluation [i.e., one listed in the Program Evaluation Plan (PEP)] in each program rather than evaluating everything. The Department of Finance have indicated that each program has been the subject of at least one evaluation of a major aspect of its functions. However, they judged that only six portfolios had achieved comprehensive coverage up to the 1992 PEP round. Two portfolios were characterised as having "non-comprehensive sprinkle across a range of programs," and the remaining ten fell in between.

In the light of this experience, the evaluation study concluded that it would be useful, from the 1993 PEP round onwards, for less ambitious requirements to be prepared on what should be expected of agencies regarding evaluation coverage in the future.

Source: Task Force on Management Improvement 1992: 378

---

ing the fact that formal program goals can differ from those of some stakeholders, and that in reality program objectives often reflect choices which have to be made between irreconcilable interests. There have been increasing demands that the users of services should be involved in evaluation coverage (Mark and Shotland 1985). These calls for greater user involvement have been taken up by the World Bank, which has in recent years given greater prominence to participatory evaluation and the role of civil society (Naryan 1993).

Such calls for evaluation coverage to give greater prominence to the user perspective have been mirrored by recent developments in public service management provision that have emphasized a move towards a customer and client focus in the public service (Barzelay 1992). Such moves are encouraging a greater involvement of users in evaluations. In the United Kingdom, for example, evaluation of community care provision has given greater emphasis to the user perspective (Barnes 1993).

There is, therefore, a trend to extend evaluation coverage of targeted objects, by increasingly including a user or consumer perspective in evaluation studies. However, as Knox and McAlister (1995) indicate, this trend raises certain issues such as how is the user to be defined? What is the value of the user input? And at what stage and level of the process is their impact most useful? They also indicate that there can be significant resource implications in building in a user perspective: resource intensive interviews with users and participant observation are often an integral part of research methods; in order to ensure representative and external validity, sample sizes have to be sufficiently large; the incorporation of user views requires particular expertise and resource skills on the part of the evaluator (Knox and McAlister 1995: 443).

What Types of Evaluation Should be Carried Out and When

The types of evaluation may be classified into six categories (Chelimsky 1985: 9–11; ERS Standards Committee 1982: 8–11):

1. *Front-end analysis.* This approach involves evaluative work that is normally done before deciding to move ahead with a new program. Typically, front-end analysis primarily addresses policy formulation types of questions, using prior evaluation findings as well as extant data to estimate likely program feasibility and effects.
2. *Evaluability assessment.* This approach is used to answer policy formulation and evaluation questions by comparing a program's assumptions and activities against its stated objectives, and by asking questions about the reasonableness of those assumptions and the likelihood that the projected or actual program activities can fulfill the program's objectives. This approach also serves to determine the feasibility and usefulness of performing a later full-scale evaluation of the program's effectiveness.
3. *Process (formative development) evaluation.* This approach includes testing or appraising the process of an ongoing program in order to make modifications and improvements. This is a form of evaluation that either stands alone or is developed in combination with another type of evaluation. It is always retrospective.
4. *Effectiveness (impact, summative, outcome) evaluation.* This approach is retrospective. It seeks to find out how well a program has been working. The results of effectiveness evaluation are intended to provide information useful in major decisions about program continuation, expansion, or reduction.
5. *Program and problem monitoring.* The approach is a continuous process rather than a once-off event. Its function is to inform on problem characteristics, or to track programs or problem processes in several areas. As such, it may address either policy formulation or executive purposes. The administrative data system that develops around the program and prob-

lem monitoring effort may also be used to answer accountability types of questions via time-series analysis.

6. *Meta-evaluation or evaluation synthesis.* This approach uses findings from one or a number of existing evaluations to determine what has been learned about a policy or program. This approach is highly versatile, capable of serving all three types of evaluation purpose: accountability, policy formulation, and policy execution.

According to an overview of the literature concerning evaluation (Owen 1993: 3–24), it has been found that each of the different types of evaluation approaches considered as its targeted object of evaluation at least one of the following objects: (1) planning, (2) programs, (3) policies, (4) organizations, (5) products (or projects), (6) individuals. Policies, programs and projects are widely regarded as key target objectives for evaluation (World Bank 1994).

It is noteworthy that in those governments and institutions which are generally seen as most advanced in institutionalizing evaluation, such as the U.S., Canada, and the European Commission, a mix of evaluation approaches can be found as they are applied to a range of targeted objectives. In other words, there is a diversity of coverage. By contrast when a government puts most of its effort into one approach or one object, problems can arise with institutionalization. For example, in the case of Italy, in the 1980s cost-benefit analysis was a favored evaluation tool, and there was a legal obligation for cost-benefit analysis to be carried out as a front-end analysis for capital projects. The Ministry of Budget drew up norms to standardize the technique. In practice, however, in many instances it became a formal administrative ritual which did not influence decision-making (see Toulemonde, chapter 7, for further details).

But saying that a diversity of evaluation approaches and targets is needed is not, of itself, particularly helpful to governments wishing to institutionalize evaluation. Are there some approaches that are more common or useful than others, some targets that yield better prospects for positive results? When starting off, are there some priority areas that governments should bear in mind?

Effectiveness evaluation particularly at the policy level, while espoused as a goal in many countries, tends not to be the principal approach used or necessarily the most successful. Rist (1992) notes that only approximately 5 to 8 percent of the studies the U.S. GAO has underway at any one time are answering cause-and-effect questions. As Ballart (1996: 17) indicates in a review of Spanish evaluation practice based on cases from five policy areas: "research designs are not optimal to measure effectiveness. Instead they tend to provide pieces of information related to various issues that are also valued by public managers and overseers.... A higher order research agenda looking at fundamental relations and implicit theories in programs is not sufficiently developed. More detailed analysis of basic links between changes in programs and consequent changes in people leading to expected outcomes is necessary to check the fundamental strategic orientation of public policies." As Toulemonde (1995) indicates, many causal links are radically unevaluable and while this does not mean that effectiveness evaluation should be abandoned, it does mean that its limitations and potentialities must be recognized.

A significant growth area in evaluation practice in recent years is program and problem monitoring. As mentioned above, program monitoring is about examining whether a public program has been carried out as it is designed by addressing such issues as efficiency, accountability, and management-related matters. In Canada, a review of departmental business plans for 1995–96 indicated much more evidence than previous plans of commitments to measure and demonstrate the achievement of results (Annual Report to Parliament by the President of the Treasury Board 1995: 6) In the United States, the Government Performance and Results Act 1993 is an ambitious program to develop performance information by all federal agencies, as box 3.2 illustrates. At the local government level, administrations such as Tilburg in the Netherlands, Windsor and Maidenhead in the UK, and the City of Sunnyvale, California are held up as leading examples of program monitoring.

Program monitoring is seen as providing a basic source of data on which further evaluation coverage can be built. Holmes and Shand (1995: 563) indicate that program monitoring "can provide improved information relevant to decision-making. It can usefully inform the budget process without a pretense that there can be a direct link between the budget and performance. It may also provide useful accountability information for public debate."

Constraints on the Institutionalization of Evaluation in Terms of Evaluation Coverage

There are several constraints apparent in the examination of different countries' institutionalization of evaluation, from the perspective

> **Box 3.2: Types of Evaluation under the Government Performance and Results Acts of 1993 in the United States**
>
> The Government Performance and Results Act (GPRA) seeks to fundamentally change the focus of federal management and accountability from a preoccupation with inputs and processes to a greater focus on the outcomes that are being achieved. A focus on outcomes—in essence, a return-on-investment in federal programs—is especially important in the current environment in which the federal government faces severe and continuing budget pressure.
>
> GPRA establishes a legislative framework for having agencies set strategic goals, measure performance, and report on the degree to which goals were met. GPRA requires each agency to submit (1) to the Office of the Management and Budget (OMB) and Congress a strategic plan by September 30, 1997, covering at least 5 years for the agency's program activities; (2) to OMB, an annual program performance plan, beginning for fiscal year 1999; and (3) to the President and Congress, an annual program performance report, beginning in 2000, covering the previous fiscal year.
>
> Congress recognized that implementing the changes required by GPRA would take time. Thus, GPRA's goal-setting, performance measurement, and performance reporting requirements are being piloted in a number of programs and agencies during fiscal years 1994 through 1996 before they are to be implemented government wide in September 1997.
>
> *Source:* GAO (1995)

of evaluation coverage. First, department resistance is a major constraint in deciding what is to be covered in evaluation. As long as responsibilities for program evaluation are delegated to government departments and executive agencies, it is natural to expect that what is to be evaluated is at the discretion of the chiefs or deputy chiefs of departments. Therefore, no one can anticipate that desirable evaluation coverage will be formulated unless the chief or deputy chiefs agree and cooperate with evaluation units of the departments or other evaluation authorities (see also Mayne, Divorski, and Lemaire, chapter 1, and Toulemonde, chapter 7 for further discussion on overcoming resistance to evaluation at the program level in departments).

Second, cabinet committees such as the Treasury committee and the policy committee in Canada, or central evaluation management organizations such as the Department of Finance in Australia, can be factors affecting decision-making on evaluation coverage. The priority for evaluation indicated by the organizations could be incompatible with that of the departments and/or agencies responsible for program evaluation. In these cases, there is no alternative to resolve the incompatible priorities but adjustment of the initial priority schedule of the department and agency involved.

Third, legal or institutional arrangements for setting up evaluation coverage do not appear to be important constraints on decisions about what is to be covered in evaluation. Until now, most of the countries under consideration have not prepared these arrangements. In other words, no specific regulations on what should be covered in program evaluation have been set up. What is to be evaluated seems to be left at the discretion of the evaluation authorities.

Fourth, and relevant to the third constraint, the number of stakeholders apparently has a great impact on what is to be evaluated. Regardless of the country, there is a wide range of actors usually involved in evaluation practices, including government departments, executive agencies, users of the services, and sometimes government organizations (e.g., public enterprises). Under these circumstances, to satisfy these diverse groups, the scope of evaluation cannot help but cover a fairly wide range.

Fifth, availability of resources, including timeframe, expert personnel, necessary materials such as the appropriate budget, and pertinent information are essential factors influencing evaluation coverage (see Toulemonde, chapter 7). Among other factors, the availability of resources can significantly affect the possibility or demand for expanding the scope of evaluation. No matter how strongly diverse groups want to see their interests or perspectives included in evaluation, the evaluator cannot cover all the objects, unless it is feasible financially or in terms of other resources.

Sixth, political constraints may be important factors influencing decisions on evaluation coverage. In particular, as a client or customer of evaluation information, the legislative branch of government appears to play an important role in stimulating evaluation capacity development in terms of evaluation coverage.

Seventh, technical or methodological constraints affect decisions on what can be evaluated. Even if departments and agencies in the central or federal government are responsible for evaluation and can wield power to decide on the scope of evaluation, it is meaningless to choose a certain target for evaluation unless appropriate analytical methods or techniques are available internally or externally through outside experts.

Eighth, constitutional arrangements for evaluation can be significant factors having an impact on decisions about what is to be covered in evaluation. In the cases of Canada, Australia, and the Netherlands, differences in constitutional arrangements for evaluation result in differences in evaluation practices; what is given priority in evaluation is already partially determined. Therefore, decision on evaluation coverage should be compatible with particular constitutional arrangements for evaluations in individual countries.

Conclusions

There are several key conclusions that result from this brief look at evaluation coverage.

First, concerning where to start with evaluation coverage, there would seem to be few hard and fast rules. It is possible to attempt comprehensive coverage across the range of government activities, or to focus on one sector and aim to get things right there. However, it is clearer when one puts the question where not to start: focusing on evaluating individual projects or programs, or devolving evaluation responsibility to ministries or departments will not result in substantive evaluation coverage. If evaluation coverage is to be institutionalized, it must be comprehensive coverage of a sector or extensive range of government functions.

Second, if comprehensive evaluation coverage is to be successful, it needs strong central support from central government bodies such as the Department of Finance and Auditors Offices which facilitate evaluation planning. This encourages the regular periodic evaluation of the activities under scrutiny. The center should also provide a coordinating role and provide guidance and advice.

Third, there is evidence in recent years of a move in several countries and intergovernmental bodies toward wider participation in evaluation by the different stakeholders, and in particular the increased involvement of service users in evaluation. User-focused evaluation and the inclusion of users views is a significant addition to evaluation coverage.

Finally, there is also evidence of a move in evaluation coverage towards a greater focus on program monitoring. Program monitoring efforts are being encouraged by governments, and are increasingly forming the basis for much evaluation-related activity. More importantly, program monitoring can supplemented impact analysis. It can provide the evaluator with a way of explaining why a program being evaluated has failed to achieve its goal(s).

References

Annual Report to Parliament by the President of the Treasury Board. 1995. *Strengthening Government Review*, Ottawa: Treasury Board of Canada.

Australian National Audit Office. 1992. *Auditing Program Evaluation*. ANAO Performance Auditing Guide.

Barnes, M. 1993. "Introducing New Stakeholders—User and Researcher Interests in Evaluative Research". *Policy and Politics*, 21, 1, 47–58

Ballart, X. 1996. "Spanish Evaluation Practice versus Program Evaluation Theory: Cases from Five Policy Areas." Working Paper, Universidad Autonoma de Barcelona.

Barzelay, M. 1992, *Breaking Through Bureaucracy*. Berkeley: University of California Press.

Boyle, R. 1997. *Evaluating Public Expenditure Programmes: Determining a Role for Programme Review*, Committee for Public Management Research Discussion Paper No. 1. Dublin: Institute of Public Administration.

Chelimsky, E. 1985. *Program Evaluation: Patterns and Directions*. New York: The American Society for Public Administration.

Commonwealth of Australia. 1991. *Implementation of Program Evaluation—Stage 1*. The Auditor General Audit Report No. 23. Canberra: Australian Government Publishing Service.

ERS Standards Committee. 1982. "Evaluation Research Society Standards for Program Evaluation." In *Standards for Evaluation Practice* (ed.). P.H. Rossi. San Francisco: Jossey-Bass, 7–20.

GAO. 1995. "Managing for Results: Status of the Government Performance and Results Act." GAO/T-GGD-95–193.

Holmes, M. and D. Shand. 1995. "Management Reform: Some Practitioner Perspectives on the Past Ten Years." *Governance*, 8, 4, 551–78.

Knox, C. and D. McAlister. 1995. "Policy Evaluation: Incorporating Users' Views." *Public Administration*, 73, 413–36.

Mark, M.M. and R.L. Shotland. 1985. "Stakeholder-based Evaluation and Value Judgments." *Evaluation Review*, 9, 5, 605–26.

MEANS. 1993. *Methods to Give Meaning to the Evaluation Obligation: The Conclusions of the MEANS Programme*. Brussels: Commission of the European Communities, D.G. XVI/02.

Naryan, D. 1993, *Participatory Evaluation*. World Bank Technical Paper No. 207. Washington, D.C.: World Bank.

Olson, J.P. 1996. "Policy and Program Evaluation." A written reply to the letter inquiring of the Office of the Comptroller and Auditor General about evaluation practices in the public sector in New Zealand. File Ref No: ERO5-0001, April 30.

Owen, J.M. 1993. Program Evaluation: *Forms and Approaches*. St. Leonards, NSW, Australia: Allen & Unwin.

Pollitt, C. 1993. "Occasional Excursions: A Brief History of Policy Evaluation in the UK." *Parliamentary Affairs*, 46, 3, 353–62.

Rist, R.C. 1992. "Program Evaluation in the United States General Accounting Office: Reflections on Question Formulation and Utilization." In *Advancing Public Policy Evaluation: Learning from International Experiences*, ed. J. Mayne, M.L. Bemelans-Videc, J. Hudson, and R. Conner. Amsterdam: Elesevier Scientific Publishers.

Rossi, P.H. and H.E. Freeman. 1993. *Evaluation: A Systematic Approach*. Newbury Park, CA: Sage Publications.

Rowe, B.J.D. 1983. "Program Evaluation in the Public Sector: Annoted, Bibliographic Review of Resources Addressing the Evaluation of Human Service and Public Program Delivery." *Public Administrative Series*: Bibliography, p. 1147.

Smith, M.L. 1981. *Federal Efforts to Develop New Evaluation Methods*. San Francisco: Jossey-Bass Inc.

Task Force on Management Improvement. 1992. *The Australian Public Service Reformed. An Evaluation of a Decade of Management Reform*. Canberra: Australian Government Publishing Service.

Toulemonde, J. 1995. "Should Evaluation be Freed from its Causal Links? An Answer Based on European Economic Development Policies.". *Evaluation and Program Planning*.

The World Bank. 1994. "Report of the Evaluation Capacity Development Task Force." Washington, D.C.: World Bank, June 30.

Part 2

Evaluation Linkages

4

Linking Evaluation With Strategic Planning, Budgeting, Monitoring, and Auditing

Per Oyvind Bastoe

In this book we regard evaluation as an essential function in public administration. Evaluation can be used in different ways—as a management tool, as a means for democratic dialogue, as a tool for control and a tool for learning—depending on who commissions the evaluation, the object of the evaluation and who uses the results of the evaluation. Evaluation is, however, not the only tool that can be used this way. Strategic planning, budgeting, monitoring and auditing are other important public sector functions that can be used for management, dialogue, control, and learning. This chapter is about the links between evaluation and these other functions.

The different functions can be applied at different stages of the life cycle of a program or policy. The life cycle can be described as a process from input to output and outcome as shown in figure 4.1. The figure shows in a schematic way how the different functions discussed in this chapter fit together in the process. The different functions serve different purposes and fit together in the process. Strategic planning and budgeting are planning instruments while monitoring and auditing are instruments for assessing what is actually happening. Evaluation can serve as the feedback loop, linking information on results with the formulation of objectives and thus be a valuable instrument for a government organization that has an ambition to influence the output in society through political programs and activities.

When trying to understand evaluation practice in a specific country or government, it is necessary to take into account the institutional context within which evaluation takes place. Evaluation findings are not

FIGURE 4.1

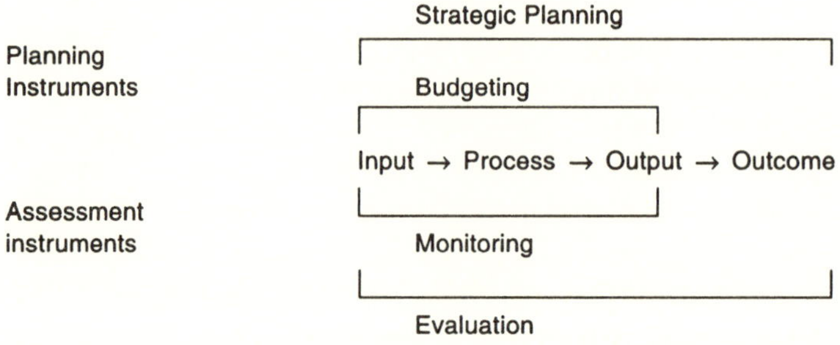

Strategic Planning

Planning
Instruments

Budgeting

Input → Process → Output → Outcome

Assessment
instruments

Monitoring

Evaluation

automatically fed back into a receptive and responsive decision-making process. Institutional arrangements determine whether or not evaluations play a part in the policy cycle, are systematically linked with other functions or carried out on an ad hoc basis. Linking evaluation to the decision-making process and to other functions is a necessary but not a sufficient, condition for using evaluation findings. A recent case study of budgeting, auditing, and evaluation in seven Western nations illustrates this (Gray, Jenkins, and Segsworth 1993). The most critical factor for the survival of an evaluation function is of course that it proves to be useful. Evaluation must add something to the process or function to which it is linked. A problem hampering the development of evaluation capacity in many countries is a lack of interest and commitment to the evaluation function at the political level. This attitude is often manifested at the bureaucratic level, and also in the lack of feedback mechanisms for applying evaluation findings. This results in both a lack of demand for evaluation results and a lack of institutional links between those who carry out evaluations and those who need to use the findings (World Bank 1994a).

The two main questions discussed in this chapter are: what are the advantages of linking evaluation with strategic planning, budgeting, monitoring and audit and what are the problems associated with linking evaluation to these functions. In the conclusion we will also discuss integration of the different public sector functions into a coherent performance management system.

Our main focus is the central government level, and the basis of the discussions will be the functions at this level. But all the functions can be used at different levels from the central government level to the local authority level, in large organizations and in small organizations.

Linking Evaluation and Strategic Planning

Strategic planning can be defined as long-term and comprehensive planning (for a period of three to five years) the purpose of which is to prepare the organization for future conditions and bolster its ability to adapt and achieve results (Statskonsult 1994.) The results of strategic planning are priorities and decisions. Strategic planning can be carried out at governmental level or in a public organization. The word *strategy* originated in ancient Greece, where strategies were selected each year to administer military matters and conduct foreign policy. Consequently, the concept of strategy has primarily a military background and association. Today the concept is generally used to denote working methods for and execution of plans aimed at achieving certain objectives. Chess is a good example of strategic thinking and execution. A chess player has to be able to analyze the expected direction of the game, including trying to predict his opponent's moves as a basis for his own moves. Strategy in this case is to envision the totality (Bastøe and Dahl 1995).

Understood in the same way, organizational strategy concerns both how an organization tries to predict development and how it utilizes and develops its aggregate resources such as finances, personnel, facilities, and the like in order to achieve future goals. Strategic planning focuses on both the individual elements in an organization, and the interplay between these elements in the achievement of common goals.

Governments try to strengthen their strategic capacity to guide the evolution of the state and to respond to internal and external changes. Strategic planning is an exercise involving rising above the day-to-day work and analyzing the challenges for the organization. Many of the ongoing government reforms help to strengthen the capacity to provide long-term perspective. Government organizations need to be proactive as well as reactive. Zapico-Goñi (1993) proposes that in times of change and uncertainty the finance ministry should guide the improvement of strategic budgeting capacities of departments and agencies, rather than just planning and programming spending. Examples of this are New Zealand departments which prepare annual strategic plans that include performance targets for the following year. The plans describe a department's mission; desired outcomes; significant issues affecting performance; the outputs to be produced at the agreed cost, quantity, and quality; management goals; and financial goals (United States General Accounting Office 1995).

Central to the New Zealand strategic planning system is the setting by government of Strategic Result Areas (SRAs), linked to Key Result Areas (KRAs) specified in performance agreements between heads of government departments and ministers (Pallot and Ball, 1996). These SRAs and KRAs can provide a useful basis for evaluation, as they aim to define objectives and outputs in a systematic and comprehensive manner, clarifying what it is the government wishes to achieve.

Evaluation can also facilitate strategic planning. The first phase in a strategic planning process is often an analysis of the current situation, to get an understanding of what is working well and what needs to be changed. Evaluation studies can help answer these questions. The involvement of all stakeholders is considered important for evaluators (Guba and Lincoln 1989). This provides a nuanced picture of the current circumstances. Careful analysis of the costs and benefits of existing policies is a key to informed, tough-minded, policy analysis and formulations (World Bank 1994b). The next phase of the strategic planning process is an analysis of the most probable development trends in the coming years. In this analysis it can be useful to use current trends and development directions as a basis. In the third phase, the consequences for the government and the public organization should be analyzed. Ex-ante evaluation, which is used to assess the case for new programs or extensions of existing programs, can be used in this analysis. This phase results in priorities and decisions.

Because evaluation often has a retrospective approach and strategic planning has a prospective approach there are obvious limitations in the extent to which these two functions can be linked. Strategic planning involves trying to anticipate the future and influence changes in the environment. Anticipating involves awareness of possible discontinuities in trends and developments. This does not mean just figuring out the future by forecasting and quantitatively extrapolating economic and demographic trends, but also carrying out future oriented qualitative research.

The main purpose of linking evaluation and strategic planning is that evaluation can provide a good basis for planning through providing data about previous and ongoing programs and policies. Without a good basis, strategic plans are likely to be unrealistic and vague. The U.S. Government Performance and Results Act (GPRA) of 1993 requires that agencies make strategic plans for a period of a minimum six years, revised and updated at least every three years (Groszyk 1996). One of the requirements in the Act is to include in the strategic plan a

TABLE 4.1
Linking Evaluation and Strategic Planning

Advantages	Problems
Evaluation can be used to analyze and understand the present situation.	Evaluation will primarily tell about the past, giving background and providing experiences for new actions.
Evaluation can be used to systematize past experiences and clarify possible decisions.	
Evaluation can be used to make consequence analysis of plans on the basis of previous experiences.	Planning is primarily an instrument concerned with the future.
Evaluation can provide necessary information in most stages of the planning process.	Plans need to have clear objectives to be evaluated.
Strategic plans can give background for evaluations to come.	

description of program evaluations used, and a schedule for future evaluations. This may be seen as a welcome and innovative feature, attempting to close the planning-implementation-feedback policy loop (Boyle 1996). This is another way of linking evaluation and strategic planning. Table 4.1 summarizes these points.

Linking Evaluation and Budgeting

The budget is the economic response to political decisions, and is the principal mechanism whereby governments give effect to their economic and social priorities. It can also be viewed as a multipurpose document resulting from multifunctional activity in the political process. Just as budgets serve planning, coordination, control and motivation in the management of public policy at the most basic level, the budgetary process acts as a mechanism for integrating differentiated interests into the regularities of the political process (Gray, Jenkins, and Segsworth 1993). A comprehensive budget facilitates: (a) measurement of the economic consequences of government actions; (b) control of the financial resources of the government; (c) accountability of decision makers and managers in the public sector; and (d) the efficient use of public resources (OECD 1995b).

In several governments there have been initiatives in recent years to improve the budget as a useful instrument of policy. The principal objective of many of the budget reforms is to encourage a greater focus on performance and results. The view that economic efficiency depends on the effectiveness of the public programs and policies has led to reappraisals of how public tasks are carried out and how performance and results are measured. This reappraisal has pointed in three closely related directions: the measurement of performance, the freeing up of managerial discretion and initiative, and the use of the budget as a means of improving results. In New Zealand, for example, appropriating and budgeting by outputs, rather than by aims, objectives or programs, is now the norm (Pallot and Ball, 1996). The aim here has been to facilitate the more transparent application of public expenditure. In many countries, proposals such as defining objectives, identifying responsibilities for results, and developing management information systems and accountability are being outlined and addressed. These improvements require strengthening the existing financial management capacity in spending departments, developing cost-consciousness and strengthening the competence and capacity in performance measurement and evaluation.

Generally speaking, the budget process includes three phases: (1) budget preparation and proposals; (2) decision by the parliament; and (3) implementation of the budget. Budgeting and evaluation can be linked in different ways in the different phases of the process.

In the first phase, when starting the budget process, evaluations can be used to answer the question about needs which are not being met at the present. Formative (process) evaluation is concerned with analyzing the efficiency of program operations, processes and procedures in relation to the program. This type of evaluation can be used to answer questions like: "Are we using the best techniques to achieve the objectives that we have identified?" Other questions concern the results of the program or activity: "How efficiently are government revenues being spent? Will shifts in budgetary allocations increase efficiency?" Outcome evaluation, which is concerned with assessing whether programs or program elements are effective in achieving what they were set up to achieve, can be used to answer these questions (Sedgwick 1993). Evaluation can also support the process by providing information about results of previous budget proposals and thus indicate possible merits and demerits of the different proposals put forward. The Australian government's evaluation strategy is an example of this way of linking evaluation and budgeting. The overall objectives of the strategy are to provide better information to program managers, to assist the government's decision-making, particularly in the budget process, and to provide better accountability to parliament and the public. In 1992 the Department of Finance carried out a survey of the extent to which evaluation findings were relied on in the 300 new policy proposals and savings options put forward to the Expenditure Review Committee of cabinet for consideration. The survey found a substantial reliance on evaluation findings in the budget process: of the 200 new policy proposals, 47 percent were influenced by evaluation findings. For two-thirds of these the influence was "direct" (i.e.,the proposals resulted directly from the findings of an evaluation). For the remaining one-third it was "indirect" [i.e., the evaluation results either provided a source of background material for the proposal or helped to create a persuasive climate of opinion (Mackay 1992)].

In the second phase, the decision-making process, evaluation of previous proposals, ongoing and completed programs and policies, can act as an input to the decision makers. The model outlined in the Financial Regulations in the Norwegian government can serve as example of this feedback to decision makers. The model entails that the Government and the Parliament draw up in the budget the overall requirements and the framework of conditions for central government agencies, including grant schemes and other instruments. The overall requirements are made operative through dialogues between the Ministries and their subordinate agencies, partly by agreeing on strategic adjustments, partly by entering into as concrete as possible agreements concerning the delivery of products and services. This is formalized in the letter of allocation, by means of which the Ministry communicates the requirements regarding goals and performance together with the annual budget for the agency. Agreement is also reached concerning the agency's follow-up of the letter of allocation by reports and analyses. The essential features of the system consist of the management dialogue between the Ministry and the agency and the Ministry's presentation of the final result of the dialogue in a letter to the agency. In the agency-internal plan of operations, responsibilities are distributed between the various organizational units, at the same time as resources are allocated and time limits are fixed. The agency is required to report back to the Ministry on its implementation of the letter of allocation, and is also required to develop the necessary financial and reporting systems for this communication. The Ministries collate the reports from their subordinate agencies, carry out supplementary evaluations and analyses, and report to the Parliament on the efficiency of institutions, grant schemes and instruments. These reports to the Parliament are made as part of the Budget Propositions.

The third phase covers the implementation of the budget. The budget is rarely implemented in exactly the form that was prepared by the legislature. Changes intrude, whether because of shifting economic or political conditions or because of numerous small adjustments in the details of expenditure. Yet as the authorized plan of expenditure, the budget must be put into effect paying due regard to the commitments or expectations established by it and the rules and limits enacted by Parliament. Implementing the budget thus requires a balance between adaptation to changing circumstances on the one hand and adherence to statutory and other strictures on the other. How this balance is struck varies greatly. There is usually provision for supplementing expenditure, whether through additional appropriations or through the transfer of voted funds from one use to another. Measurement and evaluation rarely play any dominant part in the implementation of the annual budget. Many countries, however, regularly match the spending outturn against the plan, so that appropriate and timely corrections may be made when variances emerge. In some countries there is close linkage of budgeting and accounting systems, not only to ensure that the two are on a consistent and uniform basis, but also to sensitize managers to the financial implications of their actions.

Studies (GAO 1995, OECD 1995a) indicate that the linkage between resource allocations and measurement and evaluation has proved to be difficult to apply in many countries at different levels of government. Difficulties include the limited scope of performance measurement and limited willingness to evaluate program effectiveness. Stakeholder's willingness to use the evaluations is an obvious precondition of linking evaluation and budgeting. In discussing this in a previous study by the IIAS working group of policy and program evaluation, Gray concludes that "you can drive horses to the water, but you cannot make them drink, that is, even if there are formal feedback mechanisms, they will not work unless decision makers are willing to make them work (Gray, Jenkins, Segsworth 1993). It is also important to underline that there never are automatic or mechanistic links between these functions. Evaluations can influence budgeting, not determine it.

Budgeting and evaluation can be linked in different ways and in different stages of the budget process. Evaluation can be used to point

TABLE 4.2
Linking Budgeting and Evaluation

Advantages	Problems
Evaluation provides information about the reality the budget is supposed to influence.	Budgeting and evaluation have different functions and rationale.
Evaluation can be used to analyze needs.	Evaluation might have a different timeframe than the fiscal year the budget covers.
Evaluation can be used to provide information on proposals.	
Process evaluation can be used to analyze program operations, processes and procedures and how efficiently they relate to the program.	Budgeting is prospective and closely linked to political decisions, while evaluation is largely retrospective and focuses on empirical data.
Evaluation gives feedback on how successful the budget priorities are implemented.	
Outcome evaluation can be used to analyze results of the budget allocations over time.	

at needs, to provide information on proposals, to analyze processes and to get information of the results of the budget spending. But linkage is far from automatic. Table 4.2 summarizes this section.

Linking Evaluation and Monitoring

Results of government programs and services are monitored in different ways. Performance monitoring is normally concerned with inputs, with intermediate outputs or throughputs, and with short-term or immediate outputs. It does not address long-term outputs, much less outcomes (Cave, Kogan, and Smith 1990).

A core of ideal characteristics for performance measures has been identified as being consistent over time and between units, and comparisons should be made only with similar programs. These comparisons should be simple, well-defined, and easily understood, and should emphasize those aspects that are important to decision-making. Ideally, emphasis should be given to a limited number of key measures which reflect the purpose or objective of the program or signal whether the program is worth continuing. It is fundamentally important that managers' performance should only be monitored in those areas that are under their control. It is also a good idea to inform managers of how the data will be used, and to avoid situations where considerable effort is expended in monitoring performance, only to see the collected data stored away without being used.

Increased effort is now being made to monitor the quality of services, especially from the standpoint of users or consumers. This emphasis reflects rising concern about the quality and cost of public services. Quality of service has several measurable dimensions: timeliness, responsiveness to consumers' needs, the manner in which the service is delivered, and the like. Quality may be measured by means of consumer (or citizen) surveys, and by other objective techniques. One advantage of using such measures is that it is a simple way of obtaining results. On the other hand, there is a clear limitation in that the focus is on measurable, quantitative phenomena.

A fundamental distinction is drawn between outputs that are the direct results of government actions and outcomes that are the changes in social conditions that result from a combination of outputs. For example, in an education program, outputs may be measured by test scores and the percentage of students advancing to a certain level of proficiency in mathematics. The outcomes may be measured in terms of the percentage of students completing schooling or advancing to higher education or employment.

Monitoring is not an exact science. It has obvious conceptual and practical limitations. In governments it is used as input in the decision-making process. But measures do not normally speak for themselves; they have to be analyzed and interpreted. One approach is to evaluate the data in relation to one or another standard. This may be done either by compiling a time series of measures or by comparing with other similar organizations.

According to Canadian policies established in 1976 and 1977, departments were to have in place the ability to measure effectiveness and report the results in both an ongoing and a periodic way. The two types of activities were to differ in their focus and use. Ongoing monitoring of effectiveness represented the compilation of program outputs and outcomes gathered on a regular basis, allowing program management to monitor the operations of the program. Periodic studies (evaluations) of program effectiveness involved a more in-depth review of whether program objectives were being met, often drawing on monitoring data in the process. For example, according to the 1993 report of the Auditor General of Canada, the objective of the government's Cape Breton Investment Tax Credit program was to promote durable employment in Cape Breton by encouraging new investors in the region. The Department of Finance evaluated the program, using a range of measures including some derived from the monitoring process, including:

- the additional number of jobs created in the region as a result of the tax credit
- the cost per job created versus the cost of other regional development measures
- value of new investment by industry as a result of the program
- the reduction in the regional unemployment disparities.

With regard to the value of new investments generated by the program, the Department of Finance determined that only 19 percent of the total new investment in Cape Breton could be attributed to the program and that the remaining investment would have occurred whether or not the tax credit had been offered. On the basis of this evaluation, the tax credit was discontinued (United States General Accounting Office, 1995).

Evaluation in this context can be seen as a supplement to performance monitoring in the way that it goes beyond the measures, assesses performance in depth, and considers the effectiveness of government policy and programs. Evaluation can be used to analyze measures, to get in-depth information and to decide the relevance of measures. Through evaluation one seeks to identify cause-effect relationships and reasons for a particular level of performance. In connection with program creation, implementation, and outcomes or impacts, evaluation can give valuable data and information (Rist 1989–90). Table 4.3 sums up this point.

Linking Evaluation and Auditing

Auditing is often defined as an independent examination of the adequacy of records, information and control systems. Audits involve legal and financial control of spending. In auditing, the criteria for judgment are known and clarified in advance. Chelimsky (1984) calls attention to the historical background of auditing and the close link between auditing and accounting. Auditing developed as a procedure for detailed checking, concerned with verification, with examining the

TABLE 4.3
Linking Performance Monitoring and Evaluation

Advantages	Problems
Evaluation can be used to analyze indicators and measures.	Measurements are made on a daily routine basis.
Evaluation can be used to give in-depth information in addition to the measures.	Evaluation needs a specific initiative, capacity and competence.
Evaluation puts measures and indicators into a wider context.	
Measures can serve as data for evaluations.	

correspondence between a matter under investigation and a model or standard of operation or performance. The scope of auditing in many countries is now extended from financial and compliance audits to value for money, comprehensive audits, and a concern for the efficiency and effectiveness of government programs. A distinction is drawn between "traditional auditing" (financial and compliance auditing) and "performance auditing" (how programs operate and how well objectives are achieved) (Moukheibir and Barzelay 1995). The basic concern is still the same; how does the "condition" under investigation compare to some "criterion" of performance?

Evaluation differs from auditing in that it is not necessarily based on known criteria, and in fact often starts with clarification of different criteria. Another difference is that auditing is essentially normative, examining the match or discrepancy between the criterion and the actual condition. The purpose of evaluation, on the other hand, is to provide empirical information of what has in fact occurred that is useful to policy makers and program managers to be aware of. Rist (1989) discusses the roles auditing and evaluation can play by looking at what kind of questions each can answer. The underlying logic of auditing is to answer normative questions to judge an existing condition against a norm or criteria. Cause-and-effect questions might be answered, but an auditors traditional approach often prevents them from systematically looking for and ruling out competing explanations. Evaluation has a wider approach and addresses essentially both descriptive, normative and cause-and-effect questions. Descriptive questions can be concerned with information about a problem or how a program is being implemented. Normative questions imply, both in auditing and evaluation, a comparison between the condition that exists and a norm or criteria. But evaluation many times goes further to explain how a condition has come to be. Cause-and-effect questions often include attempts to isolate the causal factor and involve using elaborate data collection methodologies and complicated data analysis to rule out competing explanations and spurious relationships.

The use of data sources may also differ between auditing and evaluation. Auditors rely heavily on authoritative documentary sources. Structured written questions and interviews is only a supplementary activity. The agency or department being audited is obliged to receive the auditors, to answer their questions and to respond to their conclusions. Since auditors have a coercive power, they do not rely on goodwill. The distance from program delivery often makes it difficult to access detailed knowledge regarding the working of programs. Evaluators, on the contrary, places heavy reliance on structured interviews and questionnaires, using statistical materials as a supplement. Evaluators often have a working relationship based on trust between all the participants and stakeholders. Analysis is often based on judgments made by those involved.

Both auditing and evaluation are used as means of managing accountability. The strongest contribution from auditing is on financial accountability. Evaluation can provide a basis for assessing process/efficiency and program/effectiveness accountability. The weaker and more ambiguous the criteria, the less the credibility of auditing and, vice versa (Rist 1989).

Both evaluation and auditing are retrospective. They involve systematic processes, are concerned with objectivity, and focus on relevance to users. These similarities give a basis for mutual understanding and learning. Evaluators and auditors already rely on each other's work, using some of the same methods. The distinction between the two approaches seems to be becoming less clear and precise: evaluators are using accounting methods for measuring efficiency while auditors are becoming more concerned with the results of the spending. In dealing with efficiency, auditors may function as if they were management consultants; and when they deal with effectiveness, especially in terms of policy and program matters, they may come close to becoming policy analysts or policy evaluators. A new and comprehensive definition of audit can therefore include other assessments, such as administrative adherence to prescribed rules and policies, the fairness of financial statements and performance reports as well as the efficiency and effectiveness of programs and operations (Gray, Jenkins, and Segsworth 1993).

In Spain, since 1987 the General Audit Office (IGAE) has been requested to carry out audits of budgetary programs, so that the appropriateness of the resources in relation to the objectives of each spending center can be estimated. According to the IGAE's guidelines, the objectives pursued within program auditing are:

- To determine whether the financial information is presented according to accounting principles;
- To determine whether the management of public funds respects current law;
- To evaluate whether management has been economical and efficient; and
- To evaluate the degree of effectiveness and achievement of objectives (Zapico-Goñi 1993).

As a summary of this point we can say that evaluation and auditing are different in approach but can be complementary. There is a development in the direction of more similarities between auditing and evaluation. Table 4.4 sums up how auditing and evaluation link.

A Coherent Approach to Performance

The various public sector functions and tools discussed in this chapter can be seen as parts of a coherent integrated performance management system. The different functions can be brought together in a

TABLE 4.4
Linking Auditing and Evaluation

Advantages	Problems
Evaluation and auditing can be complementary.	Evaluation assumes confidence and dialogue, while traditional auditing uses authority. It can be difficult to do both.
Evaluation can be used as a supplement to traditional auditing, to get a wider perspective.	
	Auditing is based on known criteria, evaluation is not.
Evaluators and auditors learn from each others approaches.	Auditing and evaluation often build on different data.

schematic order. This involves setting out the functions and their institutions in an interlocking structure of responsibilities and with networks of processual interrelationships. Such an arrangement would allow the processes to contribute to and draw on each other to produce synergy in the management of government. This assumes both a deliberate strategy of organizational design and a link between administrative and political forms in the policy process. Gray, Jenkins and Segsworth (1993) call this an "organizational integration," and point out that such a fundamental approach is rare in most governments.

In the OECD the different functions are seen as elements in "performance management" (OECD 1995a), which is a systematic approach to a management cycle in which: (a) performance objectives and targets are determined for programs (and in many cases made public); (b) managers responsible for each program have the freedom to implement processes to achieve these objectives and targets; (c) the actual level of performance against targets is monitored and reported; (d) the performance level achieved feeds into decisions about future program funding, changes to program content or design and the provision of organizational or personal rewards or penalties; and (e) the information is also provided to *ex post* review bodies such as legislative committees and the external auditor (depending on the latter's performance audit mandate), whose views may also feed into the above decisions.

There are obvious problems with a strict rational model of integration. It can, however, be argued that a rational approach is necessary in order to ensure systems and routines that provide the necessary coherence and structure. In the practical implementation of performance management, it is important to draw inspiration from other theories of management that concentrate to a greater degree on institutional "sluggishness," implementation problems and how learning actually takes place in organizations.

In many countries there have been initiatives to introduce various approaches to performance management. For the last decades the budgetary process has played the key role in these initiatives. In the United States, the enactment of the Government Performance and Results Act (GPRA) 1993 was an important step in shifting the focus of federal management and accountability away from inputs, such as personnel levels and adherence to prescribed processes, to a greater focus on achieving desired program results. Under GPRA, federal agencies are to implement result-oriented management reforms, such as strategic planning, establishing program goals, and reporting publicly on that progress. Also, to aid performance, agencies may request waivers from certain administrative rules to provide them with greater authority over program expenditures (United States General Accounting Office 1995).

A new set of economic regulations for the government administration in Norway was adopted in 1996. The aim was to achieve more effective control and utilization of public funds and better performance-oriented management. The regulations form the uppermost administrative document in a collective management concept. The formulation of objectives, control, and evaluation has a central place in the regulations.

A general characteristic of healthy organizations is that they have the ability to learn from experiences, from their mistakes and their successes. Experience-based learning entails that one looks back and builds on the transfer of information and evaluation of earlier experiences (Olsen 1993). A learning organization is characterized by a management and staff that are constantly concerned with internal and external development. A learning organization is also characterized by a systematic approach to integrating learning in daily work. This presupposes something more than methods and techniques. An "inner understanding" in the form of insight, values, attitudes, and personal development must be included to generate change and growth. An optimistic view is that a political system, with a concern for developing and learning, would install processes to ensure not only that these functions were developed separately but also that mechanisms were introduced to ensure their appropriate integration when and where desirable.

On the basis of experiences from different countries, it could be argued that a number of preconditions must be met or at least addressed in order to integrate the different functions (Gray, Jenkins, and Segsworth 1993). The first precondition is availability of data and personnel. Secondly, political authority is important in terms of changing and integrating systems, since this has more capacity than anything else to overcome organizational inertia at the lower levels of government. Thirdly, there needs to be a firm policy in political and administrative systems concerning the development and linkage of these activities, and the design of strategies to implement this. However, as any survey of the literature on policymaking and implementation would demonstrate, this is no easy task, especially where goals are unclear and the world is populated by organizations and groups with varying priorities and interests (see Rist, chapter 5, for a further discussion of this issue).

Some writers conclude that many of the attempts to develop a performance management system have fallen short of the expectations. Sandahl (1997) suggests that the complexity of modern society is one of the reasons for the failure. Evaluations are limited in scope and will only be able to provide a partial contribution to the information political decision makers need before taking fundamental policy decisions. Another important fact is that politicians often deal in intentions rather than in effects. It could be considered irrelevant to base a decision on result analysis.

Mayne (1986) points at the complexity of bureaucratic life as one of the reasons for shortcomings. Any system that is designed to cover all information needs—both operational and strategic—is bound to fail. A simplistic rational model is not sufficient in public administration. Mayne argues that ongoing performance information systems are best suited to serve the operational information needs, like administration and control of programs, while evaluations should primarily be seen as an input to strategic decisions. In this respect ongoing performance information systems and evaluations are not substitutes but complementary.

A lesson to be learnt from the various experiences, is not to be unrealistic as to what can be achieved by linking evaluation with other public management functions to provide a systematic approach to performance in government administration. Development of evaluation capacity is a long-term, difficult, and complex process.

Evaluation can be seen as an instrument for management, democracy, control, and learning. From a learning perspective, there is an universal perception that governments operate in a world of rapid change. They need to respond to changing demands from the public under increasing financial pressures. The model of a static, unchanging public sector is outdated. Evaluation, linked with other public sector functions, makes a powerful tool in public administration.

References

Bastøe, P. Ø. and Dahl, K.1995. *Den utviklingsorienterte organisasjon.* Oslo: Ad Notam Gyldendal.

Boyle, R. 1996. "Implementation of the Government Performance and Results Act of 1993: Commentary." Article in OECD, *Performance Management in Government*, Public Management Occasional Paper No. 9. Paris: OECD, 87–92.

Cave, M., Kogan M., and Smith R.(eds.). 1990. *Output and Performance Measurement in Government. The State of the Art.* London, Jessica Kingsley Publishers, Ltd.

Chelimsky, E. 1984. *Comparing and contrasting auditing and evaluation: some notes on their relationship.* Paper prepared for the Evaluation Research Society"s annual meeting in San Francisco October 11–13, 1984.

Drucker, P.F. 1989. *The Practice of Management.* London: Heinemann Professional Publ.

GAO (United States General Accounting Office). 1990. *Prospective Evaluation Methods: The Prospective Evaluation Synthesis.* Transfer Paper 10.1.10. Program Evaluation and Methodology Division.

GAO (United States General Accounting Office). 1995. *Managing for results. Expe-*

riences abroad suggest insight for federal management reforms. General Government Division, Washington,D.C. May.

Gray, A., Jenkins B., and Segsworth, B. 1993. *Budgeting, auditing and evaluation. Functions & integrations in seven governments.* New Brunswick, NJ : Transaction Publishers.

Groszyk, W. 1996. "Implementation of the Government Performance and Results Act of 1993." In OECD, *Performance Management in Government*, Public Management Occasional Paper No. 9. Paris: OECD, 71–86.

Guba, E.G. and Lincoln, Y.S. 1989. *Forth Generation Evaluation.* Newbury Park, CA: Sage Publications.

Mayne, J. 1986. "Ongoing Program Performance Information Systems and Program Evaluation in the Government of Canada." *The Canadian Journal of Program Evaluation.* 1, 1.

Mayne, J. and Zapico-Goñi, E. (eds.). 1997. *Monitoring Performance in the Public Sector: Future Directions from International Experience.* New Brunswick, NJ: Transaction Publishers.

Mackay, K. 1992. The use of evaluation in the budget process. *The Australian Journal of Public Administration.* 51, 4, 436–39.

Moukheibir, C. and Barzelay, M. 1995. *Performance Auditing: Concept and Controversies.* Background Paper Prepared for OECD/Public Management Service Symposium on Performance Auditing and Performance Improvement in Government, Paris, June 6–7.

OECD. 1995a. *Governance in Transition. Public management reforms in OECD countries.* Paris: Organization for Economic Co-operation and Development.

OECD. 1995b. *Budgeting for results. Perspectives on public expenditure management.* Paris: Organization for Economic Co-operation and Development.

OECD. 1996. *Performance management in government, contemporary illustrations.* Occasional Paper No. 9.

Olsen, J. P. 1993. Et statsvitenskapelig perspektiv på offentlig sektor. Article in Lægreid, Per and Johan P. Olsen: *Organisering av offentlig forvaltning.* Oslo, Tano.

Pallot, J. and Ball, I. 1996. "Resource Accounting and Budgeting: the New Zealand Experience." *Public Administration,* 74, 3, 527–41.

Rist, R.C. 1989. "Management Accountability: The Signals sent by Auditing and Evaluation." *Journal of Public Policy,* 9, 33: 355–69.

Rist, R.C. 1989–90. "Cross-National Perspectives on the Policy Uses (and Abuses) of Evaluation." *Knowledge in Society.* 2, 4.

Sandahl, R. 1997. "Performance Measurement Systems: A Basis For Decisions?" In Mayne, J, and Zapico-Goñi, E. (eds.) *Monitoring Performance in the Public Sector: Future Directions from International Experience.* New Brunswick, NJ: Transaction Publishers.

Sedgwick, S. 1993. "The Role of Evaluation in the Budget." In *Evaluation: Improving Program Performance and Decision Making.* Department of Finance. Australia.

Statskonsult. 1994. *Strategisk planlegging i staten.* Booklet.

The World Bank. 1994a. *Evaluation Capacity Development.* Report of the Task Force. Washington, D.C.: World Bank.

The World Bank. 1994b. *Lessons & Practices—building evaluation capacity.* November, Number 4.

Vedung, E. 1991. *Utvärdering i politik och förvaltning.* Uppsala, student literature.

Zapico-Goñi, E. 1993. "Many Reforms, Little Learning: Budgeting, Auditing, and Evaluation in Spain." In Gray, A., Jenkins, B., and Segsworth, B. (eds.).*Budgeting, Auditing & Evaluation*, New Brunswick, NJ: Transaction Publishers, 115–38.

5

Linking Evaluation Utilization and Governance: Fundamental Challenges For Countries Building Evaluation Capacity

Ray C. Rist *

A good definition of "evaluation quality" is technical adequacy plus use. Yet, having offered this definition, it must be noted immediately that it is not universally accepted in the evaluation community. There are many who adamantly believe that the evaluator necessarily must be solely concerned with the technical dimensions of the evaluation. Quality, from this perspective, is exclusively concerned with how well the evaluation is conducted and how well the results are analyzed and written. Any discussion of use is to shift to a discussion of stakeholders and events outside the influence of the evaluator.

But what this definition posits is that it is not possible to think about the evaluation endeavor without thinking about the ends to which it will (or will not) be put. Focusing only on evaluation quality as the sum total of its design, execution, and reporting on information gathered, that is, its technical components, begs an important question—why bother? The intended uses, whether instrumental, conceptual, or symbolic, of the resultant analysis and information must also be considered (Vedung, 1997).

It must be stated up front that moving into a discussion of evaluation utilization is moving into an area of strong passions, disagreements, and widely varying perspectives. Two of the past Presidents of the

* The views expressed here are those of the author and no endorsement by the World Bank Group is intended or should be inferred.

American Evaluation Association have gotten into a nasty public debate in exactly this area. What do we mean by "utilization" and how would we know it when we see it are but two of the points of discussion and dissention in the evaluation community now for more than twenty-five years—and the controversies show no signs of diminishing. Carol Weiss some years back wrote that there were at least seven distinct meanings to the term "research utilization" (Weiss, 1989). The different meanings are no fewer with respect to the term "evaluation utilization."

Why this lack of consensus still remains so central to the current characterization of the evaluation community is not the focus of this paper. That some of these issues will have to be addressed here is inevitable, but again, the intention is not to retrace the steps of the controversies or to find new ways to open old wounds. What we shall try and accomplish here is something quite different.

This paper shall resolutely move away from any discussion of the use (or abuse) of individual evaluations, whether by the evaluator, individual stakeholders, or clients. The unit of analysis is not the individual evaluation. Thus, we will not address how to build personal relations with the stakeholders, how to improve the graphics in individual reports so as to make them more reader friendly, how to write effective executive summaries, or how to deliver reports on time—all of which are strategies widely touted as means of enhancing the use of an individual report.

The focus, instead, shall be at the macro level—on how to bring the perspectives, the procedures, and the information generated by evaluation systems into the governance of modern day nation states. The intent shall be on examining key means by which a national evaluation system can enhance public sector management via, in the words of Picciotto, "the capacity to design and implement policy, to create a suitable environment for private enterprise, and to manage basic government services" (Picciotto, 1995:17).

Stated differently, the focus is on the difficult problem of linking the disparate worlds of political systems and evaluation systems. But it is a problem that must be addressed if there is to be a national evaluation system woven into the system of governance. The information and analysis which supports this present examination has been gathered over the past twelve years of research by the Working Group on Policy and Program Evaluation and reported in Rist (1990); Gray, Jenkins, and Segsworth (1993); Leeuw, Rist, and Sonnichsen (1994); Toulemonde and Rieper (1997); Mayne and Goni (1997); and Bemelmans-Videc, Rist, and Vedung (1998).

There is a risk in focusing on this level because the indicators and evidence of use are much more difficult to document and detail than they are at the level of the individual project. Patton (1988a; 1988b) and many others have been articulate in demonstrating the multiple ways in which individual evaluations for individual projects can be seen to be "useful." But Weiss (1989) and others have also been just as articulate in showing the difficulties in trying to discuss use at the national or federal department/ministry level where very seldom can an individual evaluation or even a cluster of evaluations be linked instrumentally to any consequential action in the political arena. As Weiss wrote already in 1982: "Rarely does research supply an 'answer' that policy actors employ to solve a policy problem." At this national level, they argue that taking an instrumental approach is not appropriate; use needs to be reconceptualized in symbolic or "enlightenment" terms.

The public sector in the contemporary nation state frequently generates extraordinary levels of information, data, and reports. Some of this material is budgetary in nature, other is managerial, and still other is the result of internal and external audits. Further information comes from the national research centers, the multiple components of multiple ministries, and all types of special task forces, commissions, and panels. The point is, quite self evident, that many contemporary societies are "information rich" in the amount of material they are producing in their public sectors.

But notably uneven across the contemporary landscape of governmental systems is the generation of evaluation information. Some governments have rather elaborate evaluation infrastructures in their ministries, others have it in their legislative branch, and still others have it in both—or in neither.

The supply side of the equation is uneven, often within a single country and definitely across countries. The same situation holds on the demand side. Bringing these two into some semblance of balance is difficult. Sustaining that balance is no less so.

For those systems which have a viable evaluation system in at least one branch of their government, it is not uncommon for this evaluation system to be generating a continuous set of evaluation reports. In other countries, the endeavor is nearly nonexistent. But there is now enough experience in enough countries to gain some pivotal "lessons learned" for those countries which are on the cusp of efforts to build evaluation capacity. Indeed, there is now at least a quarter century international experience with how to integrate evaluation into the business of governing.

Chelimsky notes (1995:4) that there are at least four means by which evaluation can be useful to the process of governance. These are:

- Synthesizing what is known about a problem and its proposed policy or program remedies.
- Demystifying conventional wisdom or popular myths related either to the problem or its remedies (Max Weber's *entsauberung*).
- Developing new information about problem or policy effectiveness.
- Explaining to policy actors the implications of the new information derived through evaluation.

Chelimsky earlier had expressed her view on the contribution that evaluation can make at this level in the following (1989:3–4):

> [O]bjective evidence becomes very important, not because it automatically reconciles conflicting perspectives about what is a good change and what is a bad one—of course, it cannot do that—but because such evidence can, at very least, bring nonpartisan understanding of the likelihood that a given change, whatever its goals, will be able to *reach* those goals. Thus, although the debate properly continues about what, according to belief and opinion, is or is not appropriate, objective evidence can supply empirical weight to that debate and can reduce hyperbole and exaggerated claims for policies and programs, can lessen the possibility of costly mistakes, and can avoid, over the longer term, the weakening of public confidence in government that must inevitable proceed from a record of failed shots in the dark.

> Objective evidence thus allows a stronger basis for predicting the success or failure of proposed changes and hence serves to protect the public from the vicissitudes of change that cannot possibly do what it sets out to do, from change with many costs and few benefits, from change for the sake of change. This, again, is important because while change often fails to bring the benefits hoped for, it always carries at least one major cost: that of disruption and discontinuity. Although this cost may not be immediately obvious in the euphoria that tends to accompany change, it is nonetheless real and sometimes ever measurable both in its collective aspect—that is, the unachieved goals of programs or research interrupted by the change—and in its individual aspect—that is, the careers, habits, security, and health of people adversely affected by or inadequately protected from the change.

The caveat to this argument is that evidence does not always exist—one way or the other. There are countless instances in the policy arena where there is no ability to draw conclusive support from the data for a particular policy direction just as there is no basis in the data that clearly refutes a particular policy direction. Indeed, in many instances there are no data at all, which should generate some caution in how fast and far one moves in a particular policy direction. The result in such circumstances is that the policy process moves in the absence of objective information.

But at the same time, not all policy is made in such circumstances of wanting it done yesterday. There are times when analysis can be brought to bear on the topic, when time does allow thoughtful assessment, and when the decision does not have to be made instantaneously. These are the instances when the opportunity does exist to bring research into the dialogue on the proposed policy and direction for governmental action. The question as to whether the proposed change will achieve its stated objectives can be examined in the light of what data speak to the present proposed direction and what data and experience speak to like efforts or objectives in the past.

There have been at least two broad perspectives on the issue of utilization vis a vis national evaluation systems. These perspectives have thus far appeared applicable to both the executive and legislative branches of national governments. One has been to address the utilization within the context of the politics of evaluation. Here the analysis is essentially along the lines that only with a sensitivity to the political arena and how information in general is used (or not) in this arena can the evaluation community try to strategically place itself as often as possible at the right time and in the right place. The shorthand way of framing this discourse is to talk about the uses of evaluation in the policy cycle.

The second broad perspective has focused on the capacity and willingness of a governmental institution to absorb new information, change its perspectives and behavior, and bring new data into its decision making process. If the market is the primarily means of bringing change into the private sector, what comparable mechanism exists for bringing change into the public sector. An evaluation system is one demonstrated means of doing so. Evaluation systems can facilitate change in the structures and processes of governing. In short, evaluation has a link to organizational learning.

The former perspective stresses evaluation vis a vis the processes, the routines, and the formal mechanisms of governmental procedures. It is thus more instrumental in its orientation, attempting to identify those opportunities for input from evaluation that can influence the policy process. The second approach suggests a more indirect or enlightenment orientation towards the uses of evaluation in national systems of governance. The emphasis is on the institutional platforms from which policy action does or does not emanate. In the end, they are realistically two sides of a single coin—any governing system needs both processes and platforms. They are not mutually exclusive. But they are not identical and for that reason deserve attention separately in the following pages.

There is no orthodoxy on how to approach a discourse on linking evaluation utilization and national systems of governance—only that how one thinks about linking evaluation and governance can be framed in at least two different ways with two different sets of emphases. Any country building a national evaluation system might well consider their own aspirations and assumptions, given the discussion of the two approaches that follows.

The Purpose of The Evaluation System— Part One: Influencing Public Policy Decision-making

Decision-making in the policy arena can be broadly characterized as occurring at two levels. The first level involves the establishing of the broad parameter of governmental action, for example, providing national health insurance, restructuring national immigration laws, or developing environmental protection strategies. At this level and in these instances policy research input is likely to be quite small, if not nil. The setting of these national priorities is a political event, a coming together of a critical mass of politicians, special interest groups, key elites, and citizens who are able among themselves to generate the attention and focus necessary for the item to reach the national agenda (Kingdon, 1995). This presence on the national agenda is not created by policy research and evaluation. Studies might be quoted in support of one or another position, but they are incidental to the more basic task of first working to get the issue on the national agenda.

Once the issue is on the national political agenda, there are possibilities for the introduction and utilization of policy research and evaluation. It is here at this second level of policymaking that the following remarks will be addressed—the level where there are concerns about translating policy intentions into policy and programmatic realities.

A framework within which the contribution of evaluation can be assessed in the policy arena is through the study of the policy cycle. The concept of the policy cycle has been addressed for more than a decade by, among others, Nakamura and Smallwood (1980); Chelimsky (1985); Guba (1984); and Rist (1989; 1990; and 1994a). The policy cycle as developed here will be discussed in three phases—policy formulation, policy implementation, and policy accountability. Each of these three phases has its own order and logic, its own information requirements, and its own policy actors. Further, there is only some degree of overlap between the three phases, suggesting that they do merit individual analysis and attention.'

The opportunities for a national evaluation system to produce useful information and analyses are thus enhanced with an understanding of the policy cycle—for each phase is differentiated from the others by distinct information requirements. The questions asked at each phase are distinct and the information generated in response to these same questions is used to different ends by different policy actors. Stated so, a central challenge for any national evaluation system is to so organize itself that it possesses the authority and independence to respond to the information needs at as many of the three phases of the policy cycle as possible.(1)

Phase One: Policy Formulation

Nakamura and Smallwood (1980: 31): define a policy as follows: A policy can be thought of as a set of instructions from policy makers to policy implementers that spell out both the goals and the means for achieving those goals.

How is it that these instructions are crafted, by whom, and with what relevant policy information and analysis? The answer to these and similar questions can provide important insights into the process of policy formulation.

As the formulation process begins, there are a number of pressing questions about the problem or condition that is of concern. Answering each question necessitates the compiling of whatever information is currently available plus the development of additional information when the gaps are too great in what is presently known. The information needs can be generally clustered around three broad sets of questions. Each of these clusters are highly relevant to policy formulation. In each of them are important opportunities for the presentation and utilization of evaluation information.

The first set of information needs revolve around an understanding of the policy issue at hand. What are the contours of this issue? Is the problem or condition one that is larger now than before, about the same or smaller? Is anything known about whether the nature of the condition has changed? Do the same target populations, areas or institutions experience this condition now as earlier. How well can the condition or problem be defined. How well can the condition or problem be measured? What are the different understandings and interpretations of the condition, its causes and effects? The issue here is one of the ability of policy makers to clearly define and understand the problem or condition that they are facing and for which they are expected to develop a response (see Box 5.1).

The second cluster of questions focus on what has taken place previously in response to this condition or problem. What programs or projects have previously been initiated? How long did they last. How successful were they? What level of funding was required. How many staff were required. How receptive were the populations or institutions to these initiatives? Did the previous efforts address the same condition or problem as what is currently understood to exist, or was it different? If it was different, how so? If it was the same, why are yet additional efforts necessary? Are the same interest groups involved? What may explain any changes in the present interest group coalitions?

The third cluster of questions relevant to the formulation stage of the policy cycle focus on what is know of the previous efforts and the impacts that would help one choose among present options. Considering tradeoffs among various levels of effort in comparison to different levels of cost is but one among several kinds of data relevant to considering the policy options. There may also be data on the time frames necessary before one could hope to see impacts. Tradeoffs between the

---

**Box 5.1: GAO Research on The Numbers of Infants
and Toddlers Living in Poverty**

In 1994, the United States Congress was considering legislation to expand the age range of children to be served by the Headstart Program, a large program designed to serve poor preschool children (ages 3 to 5). The question was one of just what were the numbers of poor children from birth to age three years that would be eligible for the program. Given all of these children had been born since the last census in 1990, there were no verifiable national data on the numbers. The U.S. Senate Committee on Labor and Human Resources asked the U.S. General Accounting Office to use a variety of estimation techniques to try and accurately assess the number of eligible children.

GAO conducted different studies using primary and secondary data to estimate this eligible population. The subsequent report to the Congress provided data to answer this key question as well as what the cost figures would be for inclusion of some portion or all of this target population in the Headstart Program, given different eligiblity criteria. These data were accepted by the Congress as the figures on which the subsequent debate and legislation were based.

length of the development stage of the program and the eventual impacts are relevant, particularly if there are considerable pressures for short term solutions. The tendency to go to "weak thrust, weak effect" strategies is well understood in these circumstances. Alternatively, if previous efforts did necessitate a considerable period of time for measurable outcomes to appear, how did the policy makers in those circumstances hold on to the necessary public and political support until the results began to appear.

There is an additional contribution that policy evaluation can make at this stage of the policy cycle, and it is that of studying the intended and unintended consequences of the various policy instruments or tools that might be selected as the means to implement the policy (Salamon, 1989). There is a pressing need within the evaluation community to ascertain what tools work best in which circumstances and for which target populations. Very little systematic policy evaluation work has been done in this area—which frequently leaves the policy makers essentially to guess as to the tradeoffs in the choice of one tool or another (cf. Rist, 1998).

Evaluations of the uses of tools in previous similar instances could be of significant help to policy makers in thinking through which tool (or tools) to propose in the present circumstances. For example, evaluation information could be informative to policy makers when deciding about whether to provide direct services in health, housing, and education, or to use the private sector with subsidies, vouchers, or tax credits. These are but three quick examples where policy evaluations of the relative impacts and utility of different policy tools could clearly inform decisions that have to be made.

In respect to this first phase of the policy cycle, policy evaluations can be useful and influential. This is particularly so with respect to problem definition, understanding of prior initiatives, community and organizational receptivity to particular programmatic and policy approaches, and the kinds of impacts (both anticipated and unanticipated) that might emerge from different intervention strategies. This information would be invaluable to policy makers. But hindrances to the use of policy evaluations include those of whether the evaluations were completed and published, whether the existing information is known to the policy community, and whether it is available in a form that makes it quickly accessible. Overcoming these obstacles does not guarantee the use of evaluations in the formulation process. But one can be strongly assured that if these obstacles are present, the likelihood of the use of the evaluation information will be drastically diminished.

Phase Two: Policy Implementation

The second phase of the policy cycle is that of policy implementation. It is in this stage that the policy initiatives and goals established during the formulation phase are to be transformed into programs, procedures, and regulations. The knowledge base that policy makers need to be effective in this phase necessitates the collection and analysis of different kinds of information than that found in policy formulation. With the transformation of policies into programs, the concern moves to the operational activities of the policy tool(s) and the allocation of resources. The concern becomes one of how to use the available resources in the most efficient and effective manner in order to have the most robust impact on the problem or condition at hand.

The literature on policy and program implementation indicates that it is a particularly difficult task to accomplish (cf. Hargrove, 1985; Pressman and Wildavsky, 1984; and Yin, 1985.) Quoting from Pressman and Wildavsky (1984: 109):

> Our normal expectation should be that new programs will fail to get off the ground and that, at best, they will take considerable time to get started. The cards in this world are stacked against things happening, as so much effort is required to make them work. The remarkable thing is that new programs work at all.

It is in this context of struggling to find ways of making programs and policies work that the data and analysis from evaluations can come into play. The information needs cluster into several areas. First, there is a pressing need for information on the implementation process, per se. Evaluations can examine the translation of policy intent into operational efforts, with particular reference to the logic and coherence of the policy intentions as they have to be taken into the field and implemented.

There is also the need at this stage to examine how the policy is understood at the different levels of the governmental system. The creation of a policy at the national level with a whole host of underlying assumptions and intentions may or may not survive to the regional levels and perhaps not at all to the local level where the effort is actually to be implemented. This ability to examine the inter-governmental nature of the policy and how the implementation rolls out in such a context is critical to any overall understanding of the success (or not) of the policy initiative.

A second cluster of questions at this stage of the policy cycle focus on the problem or condition that prompted the policy or program response in the first place. No problem or condition stands still. Deciding at one point to take action does not mean that the condition or problem will be the same when the response by the appropriate organization actually gets underway. Problems and conditions change—both before and after a policy response is decided upon. Thus the imperative for policy evaluations is to continue to track the condition, even as the implementation swings into action. Successful tracking of the problem or condition can provide important information to policy makers and those responsible for policy implementation. The persistent question is whether the present policy or program is or is not appropriate to the current condition. As the condition continues to change, the challenge is for the policy or program to stay responsive.

The third cluster of necessary policy questions during this implementation phase of the cycle focuses on the efforts made by the organization or institution to respond to the policy initiative. Here the issue is essentially one of institutional capacity to undertake the policy initiative (see Box 5.2). The policy question is whether the selected institution is one that can deliver the services and activities that are called for as part of the policy response. Time and again, policy initiatives are handed off to organizations and institutions incapable of taking on the added responsibilities. When this happens, the policy

---

Box 5.2: The Privatization of Korea's Public Enterprises

The privatization of state-owned public companies and enterprises is now a world-wide phenomenon. Whether in the former Soviet Union, Latin America, China, India, or Korea, the efforts to privatize public companies is a key aspect of the redesign of national economies. Korea has had a large public enterprise sector with a national budget 1.8 times greater than the rest of the national government. These enterprises also had a work force in 1994 of 368,000 persons—2 percent of the entire Korean labor force. Since the early 1990s, the Korean government has been interested in moving into the private sector a number of public enterprises. This was to be done via the selling off of government shares in the companies to private investors.

The Economic Planning Board in Korea was responsible for monitoring this initiative. A number of studies were carried out on the efficiency and speed with which the first targeted companies were privatized. The results of these date were used in the subsequent design of privatization initiatives for other public sector companies. A key concern of the studies was to assess the capacity of the existing companies to manage their own transition and compete subsequently in the private sector.

can not be well executed. The subsequent impacts are often weak, if not non-existent. Assessing capacity before the decision is made to add responsibilities to any institution can help reduce the possibility of later failure.

A final cluster of information needs at this stage build on the previous focus. Here questions are not so much on capacity as on the nature of the response, once taken. Concerns should focus on: the expertise and qualifications of those responsible for the implementation effort; the interest shown by management and staff in careful implementation; the controls in place regarding the allocation of resources; the organizational structure and whether it adequately reflects the demands on the organization to respond to this initiative; what means existed in the organization to decide among competing demands; the strategies the organization used to clarify misunderstanding or ambiguities in how it defined its role in implementation; and finally, what kinds of interaction information or feedback loops were in place to assist managers in their ongoing efforts to move the program towards the stated objectives of the policy. It is information of precisely this type on the implementation process that Robert Behn (1988) states is so critical to managers as they struggle to "grope along" and move towards organizational goals.

Phase Three: Policy Accountability

The third stage in the policy cycle comes when the policy or program is sufficiently mature that one can address questions of accountability, impacts, and outcomes. Here again, the information needs are different from the two previous stages of the policy cycle. The contributions of evaluation can be pivotal in assessing the consequences of the policy and program initiative. Just as the questions change in focus from one part of the policy cycle to another, so too does the focus of the policy evaluation research necessary to answer these same questions.

First, there is the matter of what the program or policy did or did not accomplish: were the objectives of the program met? Policy evaluation can help specifically in this regard by addressing the fundamental question of cause and effect. There may well have been many changes in the problem or condition over the length of time that the policy was operational, but it is not self-evident that those changes were caused by the policy. Many other factors could have impacted upon the condition or problem to bring about the noted changes.

The challenge for the evaluator is to parcel out what changes in the condition were caused by the efforts of the policy or program and which were not. This is one of the most difficult methodological challenges that faces an evaluator. Cause and effect relations are difficult to establish in the best of circumstances. In the case of most policies and governmental programs, the circumstances are not the best for any number of reasons, not the least of which might be the lack of good data, the lack of clear documentation of the nature of the problem, the lack of clear focus in the program ("What did they really do?"), and deliberate changes in objectives for the program over time. All these factors can hinder the ability of the evaluator to ascertain what impacts the policy or program actually had on the condition.

When a program or policy reaches the stage that it is appropriate to discuss and assess impacts, the use of evaluation strategies can offer information on both anticipated and unanticipated outcomes, changes in the understandings and perceptions as a result of the efforts of the policy, the direction and intensity of change that results from the policy, and the strengths and weaknesses of the administrative/organization structure that was used to operationalize the program. Well crafted evaluations can also be explicit about the measures being used to assess impacts and program influences. The decisions on how to measure cause and effect are tightly woven with decisions on what to measure.

There is an additional dimension to this aspect of policy evaluation that bears mention at this point. This has to do with whether the original objectives and goals of the policy stayed in place through implementation. One message that has come back to policy makers time and again—do not take for granted that what was intended to be established or put in place through a policy initiative will be what one finds after the implementation process is complete. Programs and policies make countless mid-course corrections, tacking constantly with changes in funding levels, staff stability, target population movements, political support, community acceptance, and the like. The end result is that it is often difficult to say whether or not a policy was successful because that policy was in a constant state of flux. Judging the success of a constantly moving target is an extremely difficult endeavor.

Another contribution of evaluation at this stage of the policy cycle comes with the focus on accountability. Here the emphasis can add to the original concern with external impacts a concern with internal organizational processes. The evaluation effort can address such concerns as the quality of management supervision, leadership of the organization with a clearly articulated vision and goals understood by staff, the attention to processes and procedures that would strengthen the capacity of the organization to implement effectively the policy objective, the use of data-based decision making, and the degree of alignment or congruence between the leadership and the staff (cf. Rist, 1989). All of these issues speak directly to the capacity of an organization to effectively mobilize itself to provide an appropriate response to the policy initiative. If the organization is not in a position to do so, then there are clear issues of accountability that rest with the leadership.

There are clear concerns of management accountability that must be discussed and assessed whenever programs are to be re-funded or redirected. Some of these concerns deal with impacts on the problem or condition while other focus on the internal order and logic of the organization itself. It is important during the accountability phase to determine the degree to which any changes in the condition or problem can be directly attributed to the program and whether the program optimized or sub-optimized the impact it had. Likewise, it is important to ascertain whether the presence (or absence) of any documented impacts is due to the coherence of the policy formulation, or to the nature or implementation, or both. Doing so necessitates the complex assessment of what impacts can be attributed to the policy per se and what to its successful implementation.

To summarize this discussion on inserting evaluation into a political context via an understanding of the policy cycle and how it is that any item on the political agenda moves through this cycle, consider the following quote from Albaek (1989–1990: 18):

> Thus, it appears that evaluation research has ended in a theoretical dilemma. Sponsors, policy makers, and researchers more or less tacitly agree that instrumental research utilization is better than conceptual utilization, while symbolic or legitimizing utilizations are considered illegitimate. Attempts are made again and again to improve evaluation research in order to increase its utilization in the instrumental sense. However, these efforts do not agree with our knowledge of how public policy making actually goes on and can be expected to go on in the future. There is a huge amount of work to be done if this dilemma is to find a solution. A prerequisite probably is that social science stops dreaming of making public policy making rational in order for it to use social science findings. Politics is politics and will remain so no matter what social science says or hopes. A realistic assessment of how social science can be used in public policy making must take as its point of departure a sober view of what politics is and from there consider how social science can be used in a political process, not vice versa.

The Purpose of the Evaluation System—
Part Two: Influencing Organizational Learning

In the early years of the evaluation endeavor, the emphasis on enhancing utilization was via trying to reach the individual policy maker—
a rational and thoughtful person who could be convinced by evidence
and who would make solid judgments based on the merits of the available information. New knowledge would shape subsequent decision
making which, in turn, would lead to purposeful action. The relation of
information to action was presumed to be straightforward and linear. If
good information went into the governance system, good decisions
would come out. We know now that this assumption was naive and
essentially wrong.

Organizations do not digest information in a systematic and predictable way. Rather, what information or knowledge does pass through
the multiple filters in any organization and become incorporated into
its agendas, policies, procedures, and view of the world is rather unpredictable. We can no longer assume that only "good" information gets
into an organization and "bad" information is rejected. The same can
be said for "rational" versus "irrational" information or "credible" versus "suspicious" information.

The filters that organizational systems use are neither perfect nor
predictable. The result is that any organization is full of information
that is questionable on multiple counts. That an organization will use
this information because it is at hand and is part of the organization's
institutional memory leads to all sorts of outcomes, only some of which
can be understood by outsiders who do not share in a common acceptance of the filtered information. Link this constantly filtered "knowledge base" in the organization with the means of decision making and
it is quickly evident that any decision is the result of multiple contend-
ing forces, and that rational information is but one of many potential
inputs.

Leeuw and Sonnichsen (1994: 2) capture the consequences for an
organization of this process as follows:

Besides reconceptualizing the linear concept of knowledge acquisition by organizations, organizational theorists have begun to portray organizations as deficient
in-depth probing of their assumptions that drive their administrative and operational policies. Historically, organizations have not been thought to be effective at
identifying the root causes that generate their problems. They are often described
as limiting themselves to "tinkering at the margins" when confronted with a problem or crisis.

This approach to organization problem solving ensures the recurrence of similar problems since the basic cause has been neither identified or addressed. In other words, organizations are not always good learners. Organizational learning is usually not a deliberate enterprise, but an ad hoc endeavour used for problem solving. The approach results in a residual buildup of rules, polices, traditions, and cultural artifacts that affect the decision-making process and constrain the decision maker. Further, numerous entities within an organization often compete in the production of information, each with their own biases, agendas, and objectives.

Does this rather pessimistic account of how organizations (both public and private) use and abuse information suggest that any efforts to introduce evaluation information into the governance system is futile. The answer is no, but it is also the case that the complexity of governmental decision making often defies neat compartmentalization. We have sufficient understanding of the process to know that the information upon which decisions are made in governmental systems is frequently incomplete, internally inconsistent, and highly segmented. Such is the reality, Albaek would argue, of a political system. How evaluation information fits in such a system is not going to be neat and tidy. Hence, exit the rational model of decision making.

Enter, instead, the notion of organizational learning. Argyris (1982) among others has argued for some time that organizations have great difficulty in learning and seldom question the underlying causes of their own problems. Yet, if they are to improve their own performance—and this is especially relevant in this discussion to governmental organizations—they require new information and knowledge. But we have seen that they differentially digest information. This selective acquisition and discarding of information influences the capacity of the organization to learn and thus adapt to changing circumstances and demands. The more the organization is capable of self reflection, self-study, and rigorous examination of the consequences of its past actions, the more likely it is to be able to discover and correct deficiencies, adjust to new priorities, and alter existing operational tasks to ensure effective and efficient goal attainment.

Argyris (1982) defines organizational learning as the "process of detecting and correcting error." And how is it that organizations are to come to this process of continuously working on error detection and correction? Enter here the notion of evaluation. Systematic study of planned undertakings, present actions, and of past consequences are the forte of evaluation. Evaluation can nurture and enhance organizational learning in governance systems—thus leading to improved performance and successful adaptation to changing environments.

Evaluation becomes a vital tool for organizational learning and problem solving—even if partial and selective as described above.

Linking organizational learning and evaluation is not an effort at putting old wine in new bottles. This is not a back door means to reintroduce a more rational and linear model of decision making, that is, good information leads to good learning which leads to good decision making. Quite the contrary. In the understanding of organizational learning and how it is that an organization accepts or rejects new information and knowledge, evaluation is but one player among many. Sometimes it may not even be on the field. Evaluation becomes part of a web of interacting forces, sources of information, power systems, and institutional arrangements that influence governmental action.

Whether evaluation is a frequent or infrequent participant in the learning process and consequently the decision making process of the organization depends upon many factors. A number of these factors are addressed in other papers in this volume, for example, location in the legislative or executive branches of the government, degree of autonomy, degree of centralization, linkage to other governmental functions, scope of the coverage, and the level of resources, to name but six. They all revolve around the basic concept of the degree of institutionalization of evaluation in the governance system. The greater the degree of institutionalization, the greater the influence on organizational learning and thus the greater the influence on organization decision making (see Box 5.3). Derlien (1990), for one, contents that unless the governance system takes proactive steps to institutionalize the evaluation function, the occurrence and certainly the use of evaluation findings tend to be random.

Leeuw and Sonnnichsen (1994: 9) frame their interest in institutionalization as part of a twofold hypothesis:

> Our hypothesis is twofold. The first part concerns the proper design of evaluation: evaluations precipitate debate on core organizational issues when they not only ask the question "how well are we doing," but also, "does it make sense to do it, even if it is being done well?" The second part of the hypothesis concerns the element of institutionalization: properly designed evaluations will stimulate the occurrence of such debates when they are adequately managed by the organization.

Our work to date suggests that the learning which takes place in a governmental system is hard to pin down. Even harder is trying to identify the particular decision or policy redirection that can be attributed to a uniquely self-contained evaluation as a source of data or information. Organizational learning is thus to be understood as something quite

> **Box 5.3: The Dutch Procedure of "Reconsideration"**
>
> The Dutch government established in 1982 a procedure termed "Reconsideration." This procedure necessitates an evaluation review of a select number of government programs each year. The presumption behind the policy has been that the government functions should not go unexamined for long periods of time. Thus on a rotating basis every program receives a systematic evaluation of its performance, impacts, and cost effectiveness. The results of these evaluations are reported to the full Cabinet of the Dutch government. And based on this evaluation, the program in question is "reconsidered" by the Cabinet as to its utility and the level of budget support appropriate to that utility.
>
> The institutionalization of the evaluation function within the Dutch government at the very highest level (the Cabinet) has resulted in a continuous flow of information for budgetary and program decision making. In the first five rounds of this procedure, 83 programs were reviewed and reports submitted. A number of programs had their budgets cut significantly, others had increases, and one program was eliminated altogether.

other than the mastery of individual facts and data in order to sit and make a discrete decision. Organizational learning can come from many sources and via many avenues. Further, not all learning must necessarily derive from or be associated with decision-making. Decision-making is but one among the multiple activities and functions of an organization. Learning can happen in and for the benefit of any organizational function. When and how evaluation can assist in this learning is an area that needs considerable study.

From our research thus far, a short list of six preconditions can be drawn that suggest receptivity of governmental organizations to evaluation information. A discussion of each item and the rationale for its inclusion can be found in Rist (1994b).

The six are as follows:

1. Governmental organizations are more receptive to (and thus filter less of) the information generated by their own internal evaluation units than that generated by external units. The proclivity to give greater reliance and trust to information generated from within allows this information to move through the various filters and thus receive a higher level of attention and reaction.

2. There appears to be a positive relationship between the credibility of the source and the acceptance of the information. Information that comes into an organization from an outside organization that is not seen to be legitimate, or information that comes into an organization

without an legitimate inside sponsor is information that is not likely to be accepted and acted upon. The reverse also appears to hold true: an organization will accept outside information when the source appears credible, non-confrontational, and the benefits for the receiving organization are evident.

3. Organizational learning is not only dependent upon how the organization perceives the supplier of the information, but also how influential the organization perceives the internal receiver to be.

4. Interinstitutional scrutiny must be perceived as legitimate if the information is to be accepted and responded to by the receiving organization. The information generated by organizations with oversight responsibilities can have a significant, if begrudging impact on the subsequent learning and behaviour of the affected organizational units.

5. The manner in which evaluation information is shared with the relevant institution greatly affects the acceptance of the information; building of trust, contact, and channels of communication matter greatly, and it is rare that an evaluation report, simply by itself, generates organizational learning.

6. Efforts to generate learning within an organization must be constantly renewed. Nothing with respect to organizational learning stays still for very long.

In discussing the relation of evaluation to organizational learning, I summarized our thinking thus far as follows:

> Those in the policy and program evaluation communities who are interested in the improvement of government and seek to have the information they generate understood and become influential had better commit themselves for the long term. What the studies reported here suggest is that the promise of public sector learning can be fulfilled, but that it cannot be taken for granted. Change is a given, Further, chance is a given. Much has to be right for an organization to learn. But much can go wrong and then little happens. The organization perpetuates its old ways of behaving, no new information enters the system, and the system moves along until it is again confronted with the challenge/opportunity to think about itself differently. The presence of policy and program evaluation information has been established in these studies to influence organizational learning. But for the efforts to be more than episodic and erratic, a sustained commitment to producing useful information and working with the users of such information is an imperative.

A Final Note

The countries now building or reviewing national evaluation systems have a dual challenge. They have, on the one hand, to try and figure out what portion of all that we have learned from the first and second wave countries is applicable to their respective governance systems. How can they organize their own national evaluation systems to have the possibility of addressing the various information needs of the policy cycle. On the other hand, they have to undertake their own efforts at organizational learning in order to figure out the new arrangements necessary for the institutionalization of the evaluation function. Neither of these are easy. Both appear necessary.

Note

1. Material presented in this section is a revision of that previously published in Rist 1994a and Rist 1995.

References

Albaek, E. 1989–1990. "Policy Evaluation: Design and Utilization." *Knowledge in Society*. Vol. 2, no. 4.

Argyris, C. 1982. *Reasoning, Learning, and Action*. San Francisco, CA.: Jossey-Bass Publishers.

Behn, R. 1988. "Managing By Groping Along." *Journal of Policy Analysis and Management*. Vol. 7, no. 4.

Bemelmans-Videc, M.L., R. C. Rist, and E. Vedung (eds.). 1998. (forthcoming). *Carrots, Sticks, and Sermons: Policy Instruments and Their Evaluation*. New Brunswick, N.J.: Transaction Publishers.

Chelimsky, E. 1985. "Old Patterns and New Directions in Program Evaluation." In E. Chelimsky (ed.), *Program Evaluation: Patterns and Directions*. Washington, D.C.: American Society for Public Administration.

Chelimsky, E. 1989. "Evaluation and Public Policy: The Use of Evaluation Products in the Executive and Legislative Branches of the U.S. Government." Washington, D.C.: Economic Development Institute, The World Bank.

Chelimsky, E. 1995. "Preamble: New Dimensions in Evaluation." *New Directions for Evaluation*. Number 67 (Fall).

Derlien, H. 1990. "Genesis and Structure of Evaluation Efforts in Comparative Perspective." In R. Rist (ed.), *Program Evaluation and the Management of Government*. New Brunswick, N.J.: Transaction Publishers.

Gray, A., B. Jenkins, and R. Segsworth (eds.). 1993, *Budgeting, Auditing and Evaluation*. New Brunswick, N.J.: Transaction Publishers.

Guba, E. 1984. "The Effects of Definition of Policy on the Nature and Outcomes of Policy Analysis." *Educational Leadership*. Vol. 42, no. 2.

Hargrove, E. 1985. *The Missing Link: The Study of the Implementation of Social Policy*. Washington, D.C.: The Urban Institute Press.

Kingdon, J.W. 1995. *Agendas, Alternatives, and Public Policies*. New York: Harper Collins.

Leeuw, F., R. Rist, and R. Sonnichsen (eds.). 1994. *Can Governments Learn? Comparative Perspectives on Evaluation and Organizational Learning*. New Brunswick, N.J.: Transaction Publishers.

Leeuw, F. and R. Sonnichsen. 1994. "Evaluation and Organizational Learning: International Perspectives." In Leeuw, F., R. Rist, and R. Sonnichsen (eds.)., *Can Governments Learn?* New Brunswick, N.J.: Transaction Publishers.

Mayne, J. and E. Goni (eds.). 1997. *Performance Management and Evaluation.* New Brunswick, N.J.: Transaction Publishers.

Nakarmura, R. and F. Smallwoood. 1980. *The Politics of Policy Implementation.* New York: Saint Martin's Press.

Patton, M. 1988a. *Qualitative Evaluation and Research Methods.* Newbury Park, CA.: Sage Publications.

Patton, M. 1988b. "The Evaluator's Responsibility for Utilization." *Evaluation Practice.* Vol. 9, no. 2.

Picciotto, R. 1995. "Introduction: Evaluation and Development." *New Directions for Evaluation.* Number 67 (Fall).

Pressman, J. and A. Wildavsky. 1984. *Implementation.* (3rd ed.), Berkeley, CA.: University of California Press.

Rist, R. 1989. "Management Accountability: The Signals Sent by Auditing and Evaluation." *Journal of Public Policy.* Vol. 9, no. 3.

Rist, R. (ed.). 1990. *Program Evaluation and the Management of Government: Patterns and Prospects Across Eight Nations.* New Brunswick, N.J.: Transaction Publishers.

Rist, R. 1994a. "Influencing The Policy Process with Qualitative Research." In N. Denzin and Y. Lincoln (eds.). *Handbook of Qualitative Research.* Thousand Oaks, CA.: Sage Publications.

Rist, R. 1994b. "The Preconditions for Learning: Lessons From The Public Sector." In Leeuw, F., R. Rist, and R. Sonnichsen (eds.). *Can Governments Learn: Comparative Perspectives on Evaluation and Organizational Learning.* New Brunswick, N.J.: Transaction Publishers.

Rist, R. (ed.). 1995. *Policy Evaluation.* Aldershot, U.K.: Edward Elgar Ltd.

Rist, R. 1998 (forthcoming). "Choosing the Right Policy Instrument at the Right Time: The Contextual Challenges of Selection and Implementation." In Bemelmans-Videc, et al., *Carrots, Sticks, and Sermons: Policy Instruments and Their Evaluation.* New Brunswick, N.J.: Transaction Publishers, Inc.

Salamon, L. 1989. *Beyond Privatization: The Tools of Government Action.* Washington, D.C.: The Urban Institute Press.

Toulemonde, J. and O. Rieper (eds.). 1997. *The Politics and Practice of Intergovernmental Evaluation.* New Brunswick, N.J.: Transaction Publishers.

The World Bank. 1994. *Evaluation Capacity Development.* Washington, D.C.

Vedung, E. 1997. *Public Policy and Program Evaluation.* New Brunswick, N.J.: Transaction Publishers.

Weiss, C. 1982. "Policy Research in the Context of Diffuse Decision Making." In R. Rist (ed.), *Policy Studies Review Annual, Vol. 6.* Beverly Hills, CA.: Sage Publications.

Weiss, C. 1989. "Evaluation for Decisions: Is Anybody There? Does Anybody Care?" *Evaluation Practice.* Vol. 9, no. 1.

Yin, R. 1985. "Studying the Implementation of Public Programs." In W. Williams (ed.), *Studying Implementation.* Chatham, N.J.: Chatham House.

Part 3

Evaluation Capacity Building

6

Professionalizing the Evaluation Function— Human Resource Development and the Building of Evaluation Capacity

Richard Boyle

In this chapter, the focus is on the human resource element of the supply side of evaluation capacity; the need for a basic cohort of evaluators who are trained in the methodologies and management of evaluation studies. In particular, there are four main issues that are explored:

1. *Preparing the ground for evaluators.* What are the main disciplines and competencies from which the "curriculum" for evaluators is derived?
2. *Selecting, placing and developing evaluators.* How do governments select place and develop evaluators? What "profile" do evaluators have? What kind of development programs are used for evaluators, and how appropriate are they?
3. *Developing evaluation users.* How can users be encouraged to create active demand to match evaluation supply?
4. *Professionalizing evaluation.* What is being done and needs to be done to support the specialization of professionals in evaluation? What is the role of professional associations?

Preparing the Ground for Evaluators

In establishing evaluation capacity it is first of all necessary to ensure that the ground has been well prepared; that the academic disciplines necessary to foster evaluation growth are present. Derlien (1990) has indicated that a lack of scientific infrastructure hampers the institutionalization of policy evaluation. A number of disciplines have developed to provide the necessary theoretical and methodological bases for

TABLE 6.1
The Locus of Evaluation in Academic Curricula:
Examples from a Number of Countries

The United States of America

The policy sciences and public administration are key bases for evaluation. In university-based public policy institutions there is a dominance of quantitative methods and economics, policy analysis, and, since the 1980s, a renewed emphasis on management in public policy programs. Specific courses in program evaluation are offered as part of the curriculum.

Canada

The social sciences hold a strong position with regard to the teaching of evaluation. There is also an increasing predominance of economics and management. Although few institutions of higher learning offer a full range of evaluation courses, evaluation has acquired a place of its own in academic curricula, either as a subject in its own right or in relation with subjects like planning and policy analysis.

The Netherlands

In the mid-1970s, policy analysis and evaluation began to be represented in the curricula of the academic programs in public administration. Relevant training from a methodological point of view is offered in social science programs (especially in sociology), economics (cost-benefit/cost-effectiveness analysis) and policy research.

The Scandinavian countries

In Sweden, in the universities there are schools of public administration where policy evaluation is being taught. In Norway and Denmark, evaluation-related blocks are offered in courses on public administration, political science, economics and statistics. Occasionally, evaluation is taught as a subject in its own right. In Finland, modules on policy analysis, evaluation and implementation research are run in academic public administration programs, while in related modules (on financial administration and government auditing) economic analysis and auditing are covered.

Source: Bemelmans-Videc, Eriksen, and Goldenberg (1994)

evaluation. Particularly notable are the applied social sciences, including economics, sociology and psychology, political science, and public administration (Bemelmans-Videc, 1992; Henry, 1987). Table 6.1 provides examples of the location of evaluation and evaluation-related activities in academic curricula for a range of countries.

Some general trends can be determined in developments in evaluation-related curricular activities. First, in several countries, evaluation theory and methodology were originally taught mainly in the framework of training in sociology, political science, and economics. Recently, the subject is becoming a separate, standard part of curricula, especially in public administration programs. Second, there is an increased emphasis on improved *management* of the public services, in the context of increased fiscal stress, which has served to emphasize the development of policy analysis and evaluation as management tools that can be used to enhance the effectiveness of services. Academic programs in public management now vie with more traditional public administration programs. Third, the introduction of "value for money" auditing in countries such as the United Kingdom and Ireland, and comprehensive auditing and performance auditing in other countries, has increased the role of auditing in promoting evaluation activities. Evaluation is now an important element in many auditing courses and programs.

Selecting, Placing, and Developing Evaluators

Once the academic background is there to provide evaluators with the basic skills and competencies, governments must then select and place evaluators and support their ongoing development. In this section, these tasks are explored, with a view to assessing what is happening in a range of countries on these tasks, and what issues arise as a result. These issues are also explored by Sonnichsen in chapter 2, specifically in the context of internal evaluators.

Selection and Placement of Evaluators

In selecting evaluators, decisions must be made on the background and experience that evaluators should have. There are no clear guidelines from international experience here. Bemelmans-Videc, Eriksen, and Goldenberg (1994) indicate that in the United States: "a number of occupations represent the core from which higher civil servants engaged in policy analysis/evaluation can be drawn: program analyst, management analyst, budget analyst, social science analyst, operations research analyst, economist, and General Accounting Office (GAO) evaluator." However, the U.S. experience is not typical. The Bemelmans-Videc et al. (1994) study indicates that in many countries no discernible pattern emerges for the selection of evaluators. They cite a March 1990 edition of the *Program Evaluation Newsletter:* "Few people in Canada graduate...specifically as program evaluators. No single educational stream or, for that matter, no specific on-the-job experience seems to lead naturally to the practice of evaluation; evaluators came from various places, probably as it should be."

Also with regard to selection is the question of whether to look for newly qualified graduates or to aim for people with some practical experience. Much depends on the purpose of the evaluations undertaken and the type of evaluation study to be carried out. In Ireland, in an evaluation unit set up to evaluate expenditure disbursed under the European Social Fund (ESF), a key criterion for employment in the unit is relevant work experience. Experience is seen as particularly important for the credibility of evaluators going out into the field gathering data from the agencies spending the ESF money. Young graduates straight out of third-level institutions are not seen as having sufficient credibility to deal with senior managers in agencies. A background of working experience in analysis and evaluation is seen as enhancing the standing of the evaluator, and subsequently their ability to conduct evaluation studies.

Once selected, evaluators must then be "placed" in the system of government. Many of the issues concerning placement have been covered by Mayne, Divorski, and Lemaire and Sonnichsen in chapters 1 and 2. Here, the emphasis is on the human resource development implications of placement. From this perspective, three main possibilities for placing evaluators are:

1. Creating specialist evaluators and putting them in dedicated posts and/or units;
2. Encouraging evaluation skills development at the program management level;
3. Outsourcing evaluation, through specialist institutions, consultancy firms, etc.

Employing specialist evaluators in dedicated evaluation units or offices is one commonly used strategy for building evaluation capacity in government. These units may be internal or external, centralized or decentralized, with their associated advantages and disadvantages as Sonnichsen indicates in chapter 2. From a human resource development perspective, the main advantages of specialized evaluators are:

1. That they can devote themselves full time to developing and maintaining the appropriate methodological, theoretical and practical skills associated with evaluation, and
2. That as evaluations are conducted and expertise gained, there is a learning process whereby improvements are made to the evaluation process. This is a particular strength compared to the situation where evaluations are contracted out on a once-off basis to external providers, where the

experience gained is lost to the organization. In the case of specialized units, the experience gained reinforces and enhances the work of the unit.

The main disadvantage of specialist evaluators or dedicated evaluation units is that they can be seen as part of a bureaucracy and red tape which reduces the effectiveness of operational staff in getting on with their job of serving the people. In the United States, there was a significant decline in evaluation functions in central government in the 1980s, with centralization and abolition of some units (Rist, 1990). Under the Reagan administration, evaluation was seen as somewhat contrary to his philosophy of government.

An alternative strategy is to focus on developing evaluation skills at the program management level. This approach is pursued, for example, in Norway (Bemelmans-Videc et al. 1994) and Australia (Task Force on Management Improvement, 1992). The advantages here include the fact that the staff conducting the evaluations will be intimately involved with the programs and policies under scrutiny, and thus be familiar with the subject and well placed to take effective decisions based on the findings. From a human resource development perspective, however, the adequacy of skills available may be a problem, as could work overload if staff are trying to combine evaluation activities with other duties. They may also be seen as lacking "distance" and objectivity.

The third approach, contracting out evaluation studies to external evaluators, may suit governments which feel that they do not have the necessary skills "in-house," yet who wish to pursue evaluation activities. It may also provide independent evaluations. Germany and Italy would be examples where governments make extensive use of evaluators drawn from outside government departments. In Germany, for example, extensive use is made of numerous "quasi-autonomous" federal research institutions (Bemelmans-Videc, et al. 1994). A central disadvantage of this approach from a human resource development perspective is that the experience gained from the evaluations, whilst retained in the institutions, is not captured within government departments: the opportunities for learning are not systematized.

Of course, in practice these alternative strategies are not mutually exclusive, and it is common to find governments mixing the three. Where the emphasis lies will depend on the governments priorities and view of the role of evaluation. In terms of the impact on evaluation capacity development, the approach adopted and the precise mix can have significant impacts, and will need to be monitored by governments on an

---

Box 6.1: Placing Evaluators in the Australian Public Service

Agencies generally believe that responsibility for evaluation should lie with the program manager. However, the question then arises as to whether a program area is capable of carrying out the evaluations without help, and if not, what help is required. Experience varies. The Department of the Prime Minister and Cabinet mostly use in-house staff. In the Department of Immigration, Local Government and Ethnic Affairs a range of sources are used: in-house, independent peer-review, consultants, or a mixture.

The constraint on evaluation activity most frequently mentioned is unavailability of staff with relevant skills. This encompasses both (a) skills in conducting evaluations and (b) expertise in the subject matter area.

The Commonwealth Scientific and Industrial Research Organization employs different skills in different types of evaluation. For retrospective evaluations it typically uses independent professional economists to conduct cost-benefit analyses. Prospective evaluations, to determine priorities and funding proposals, tend to be done internally on a more routine basis.

The Department of Employment, Education and Training shares responsibility for evaluations between a specialist Evaluation and Monitoring Branch and the relevant program area so as to combine the expertise of program managers with the skills and independence of a specialist evaluation unit. However, even with this approach it reports that skills shortages are causing evaluations to take longer to complete than planned.

Source: Task Force on Management Improvement, 1992

---

on-going basis to ensure that the right balance is struck. Box 6.1 gives an example of the Australian experience, which reflects some of the issues considered in this section.

Developing Evaluators

The development of evaluation skills is a key task if governments are to achieve benefits from evaluation studies. Ensuring that evaluators keep their skills and competencies up to date in a rapidly changing environment is crucial for effective long-term institutionalization. In order for this to happen, evaluators must be specially trained and prepared for evaluation. There are a number of approaches that are possible.

- The use of short-term training courses. As Toulemonde (1995) points out, there are plenty of seminars and conferences targeted at practitioners and dealing with evaluation in different European countries: "However, these events rarely last for more than one or two days. They can hardly be considered as actual training and should be qualified as initiation." They give a grounding in evaluation, increasing knowledge, but are not a substantive investment in skills development.

- Building networks of evaluators sharing experience through seminars, workshops and the like. In Scandinavia, for example, a community of evaluation practitioners has developed, mainly interested in improving their know-how about evaluation methodologies. Participants include civil servants, academics and consultants (MEANS Internal Bulletin, 1995).

- The provision of longer-term, post-graduate-level programs for professional development. Often at present these are not exclusively aimed at evaluation, but will have a significant evaluation component. For example, in America many post-graduate programs in areas such as public administration, education and psychology include several evaluation courses such as evaluation theory and methodology. (Altschuld, et al., 1994).

- Central government agencies support for a range of initiatives aimed at enhancing evaluator's competencies. Examples here include (Bemelmans-Videc, et al. 1994):

  - in Canada, the Program Evaluation Branch of the Office of the Comptroller General provides a series of seminars or workshops and information exchange sessions for members of the evaluation community. These events range from orientation workshops for new members of the community to methodological workshops aimed at more experienced members.

  - in the Netherlands, the Ministry of Finance's Department of Policy Evaluation and Instrumentation offers courses in ex-ante and ex-post evaluation, publishes guidelines for evaluation, and conducts educational activities.

  - in Denmark, the Danish School of Public Administration provides training for government officials at all levels. It offers an eight week course in top-management covering subjects related to evaluation.

- Promoting the development of professional associations. Professional associations for evaluators seems internationally to be taking on a more important and active role in defining and promoting professional development. The American Evaluation Association and Canadian Evaluation Society are long-standing associations. The Australasian Evaluation Society was founded in 1986. More recently, 1994 has seen the creation of a European Evaluation Society and a United Kingdom Evaluation Society. An example of the aims and issues concerning an evaluation association are given in Box 6.2, for the Australasian Evaluation Society. Such associations can play a useful role in a number of ways. They can act as facilitator of a network of evaluation practitioners and users in the evaluation community, bringing people together for conferences, seminars and the like. They can promote good practice and raise awareness of methodological and skills developments and innovations. They can provide and promote education, training and development, fostering the growth of professional evaluators. They can be the source of the establishment and promotion of standards and ethical guidelines. In all, professional associations offer a useful support for developing the evaluation resource.

An important point to note in providing development opportunities for evaluators is to achieve an appropriate balance between enhancing

---

Box 6.2: The Australasian Evaluation Society

Aims

The aim of the society is to *improve the theory, practice and use of evaluation* through:

1. establishing and promoting ethics and standards in evaluation practice;
2. providing forums for the discussion of ideas, including society publications, seminars and conferences;
3. linking members who have similar evaluation interests;
4. providing education and training in matters related to evaluation;
5. recognizing outstanding contributions to the theory and/or practice of evaluation;
6. acting as an advocate for evaluation;
7. and other activities consistent with this aim.

Current issues

Three issues regarding "professionalization" of evaluation have been the focus of much debate in the last few years:

■ **The discipline of evaluation versus the profession of Evaluators.**

The AES has twice rejected the notion of restrictive membership or any elitist connotation of "professionalization" of evaluation as a "guild."

■ **Ethics and standards**

In 1991, the Society adopted as its policy the standards put forward by Stufflebeams' "Joint Committee on Standards of Educational Evaluation" (1981). Since the new edition of the American Standards for Evaluation by the "Joint Committee" (Chaired by Dr. James Sanders, 1994), the AES has been revising its *Interim Code of Ethics* and developing a set of guidelines on the application of these standards in Australia.

■ **Training and professional development in evaluation**

The AES has, since 1991, convened a Committee on Training and Professional Development. This Committee set up a clearing house on professional evaluation development and training, which regularly circulates information on the courses and topics available concerning evaluation around Australia and New Zealand.

(Source: News from the Community, 1995)

knowledge and skills of the "harder" quantitative methodologies and tools needed to conduct evaluation and the "softer" skills and competencies needed to manage evaluation studies. As Sonnichsen illustrates in chapter 2, for example, internal evaluators may be expected to act as change agents and advocates, whereas external evaluators may be expected to stress the objectivity and independence of their stance. Whilst both types of evaluation share the need for methodological know-how, the competencies needed to put the evaluation into practice are different. In particular, if governments are keen to promote the concept of the evaluator as change agent, they will need to ensure that change management skills are built into in-service training and development programs. Development of evaluators covers both (a) enhancing the theoretical and methodological "tool-box" of the evaluator, and (b) improving the evaluators' understanding of the managerial and political context within which evaluation takes place.

Table 6.2, derived from work by Mertens (1994) indicates the knowledge and skills base associated with evaluation. The methodological skills needed are clearly outlined, but so too are the "nontechnical" skills needed, such as interpersonal and communications skills, negotiation and facilitation. These "softer" skills are increasingly being seen as important in many countries, particularly as involving program users in the evaluation process becomes a growing element in evaluation practice. As Knox and McAlister (1995) indicate, "if the interests of service users are deemed to be paramount, this will result in a very different kind of evaluation to one in which the requirements of those funding the policy are seen as most important." Particular expertise and skills are needed on the part of the evaluator when the views of users are sought. This point has been stressed by the World Bank in a study of participatory evaluation where the role of the external evaluator is outlined:

> In addition to the technical skills they bring, participatory evaluators must also have strong skills in facilitation, as well as humility, respect for others, and the ability to listen. They must also have a strong belief in human potential and a high tolerance for ambiguity. When many people are involved in decisions and tools have to be adapted or developed to fit the local situation, decision making naturally takes longer and is less clear-cut initially than when one person or a small group is in control. (Narayan, 1993:13)

Developing Evaluation Users—Linking Supply and Demand

Thus far, the emphasis has been on investigating the skills and competencies needed by evaluators in order to facilitate successful evalua-

TABLE 6.2
Knowledge and Skills Requirements for Evaluators

1. **Knowledge and skills associated with research methodology**
   a. Understanding of alternative paradigms and perspectives
   b. Methodological implications for alternative assumptions
   c. Planning and conducting research

2. **Knowledge and skills needed for evaluation but borrowed from other areas**
   a. Administration/business, e.g., project management
   b. Communication/psychology, e.g., oral and written communications, negotiation skills.
   c. Philosophy, e.g., ethics, valuing
   d. Political Science, e.g., policy analysis, legislation
   e. Anthropology, e.g., cross-cultural skills
   f. Economics, e.g., cost benefit and cost effectiveness analysis

3. **Knowledge and skills unique to specific disciplines e.g. education, health**

4. **Knowledge and skills associated with understanding governmental functions e.g., budgeting, auditing, strategic planning**

Source: Adapted from Mertens (1994), pp. 21–22.

tion studies. However, it is worth stressing that evaluation *users* should also receive training and development support to facilitate their involvement in the process, from commissioning of evaluations through to implementation of their findings. The need is to create what Morris (1994) has termed *educated consumers* who "can articulate meaningful evaluation questions at a general level and develop evaluation designs and data collection strategies for the programs that they fund, administer, or staff. Thus, they should be able to interact effectively with those who actually evaluate these programs, and in this sense they can be knowledgeable, motivated consumers of professional evaluation services." This would be akin to the Australian experience of trying to create demand and responsibility for evaluation at the program level as exemplified in Box 6.1. It relates to the general trend in many industrialized countries to introduce a "managing for results" approach to the activities of public service organizations (Boyle, 1995).

In terms of the interaction of supply and demand for evaluation discussed in the introduction, creating educated consumers is one of the activities needed to facilitate effective demand. Users' ability to articulate what it is they want from evaluation, and to understand the strengths and limitations of evaluation, is one of the keys to effective demand.

Educated consumers can help create an evaluation "ethos," where evaluation is valued as an integral part of the governmental decision-making process. Expertise can be brought in and applied as necessary to undertake evaluations, but unless the will is there on the consumers' side to commission studies and act on the findings, such expertise is largely irrelevant.

An interesting example of a developmental initiative to support evaluation users and enhance their understanding of evaluation practice is the recent creation of a training seminar for European Commission officials involved in overseeing evaluation activity in the area of the structural policies programs. This seminar, run as part of the MEANS (Methods for Evaluating Structural Policies) program, covers issues such as evaluation's mandate; writing terms of reference; methods and techniques; and mastering the quality of evaluation (see Box 6.3).

Such developmental initiatives aim at ensuring that evaluation capacity in human resource terms is translated into actual use. They illustrate the point that organizations and governments need human resource management (HRM) policies that facilitate innovation and learning if

---

Box 6.3: Evaluation seminar for European Union Officials

Background. The seminar, held over four days, and repeated for different groups as requested, aims to provide European Union (EU) officials with responsibility for managing EU structural policies with an opportunity (a) to exchange views on the use of evaluation, and (b) learn from the experience of European and North American research into evaluation practice.

Aims. The seminar addresses several key questions:

1. How can evaluation be useful in decision-making and reorienting programs?
   - providing relevant feedback for the decision-making process;
   - facilitating shifts of resources between sub-programs and projects;
   - correcting management problems.

2. How to improve the organization of evaluation?
   - integrating evaluation with the agenda of management committees;
   - the importance of posing the right evaluation questions;
   - improving knowledge of evaluation techniques;
   - influencing the choice of evaluator.

3. How to get the most out of your evaluator?
   - improving knowledge of different types of evaluator;
   - determining their levels of independence;
   - judging the timing and the form of the publication of results.

evaluation is to be institutionalized. A key finding from the Bemelmans-Videc et al. (1994) study is that there is a strong correlation between the pace of institutionalization of evaluation and the degree to which the dominant administrative philosophies, expressed in HRM policies, are open to innovation:

> Where the administrative-legal culture is clearly dominant and HRM is hesitant (or repressed) in expressing different values and academic specialties the acknowledgment of evaluation is seriously hindered. This correspondence may indicate a conditional relationship: the clear need for HRM to support and facilitate the introduction of evaluation into central government as an innovation. (Bemelmans-Videc et al. 1994: 180)

The Bemelmans-Videc et al. study indicates that the more evaluation is seen as part of the tool kit of managers in government, the more they will be inclined to demand evaluation expertise in their organizations, thus creating a positive interaction between supply and demand.

Professionalizing Evaluation

A question many governments will face in building evaluation capacity is the extent to which the development of evaluation as a profession should be encouraged. Should there be such a creature as a professional evaluator? Such issues are being extensively debated in the United States at the moment, and have been the subject of a special issue of the journal *New Directions for Program Evaluation* [Altschuld and Engle (eds.), 1994]. The degree of professionalization of evaluation and evaluators is an important question for human resource development, as it sets the context for issues such as training and development and certification.

Worthen (1994) has put forward a list of nine characteristics which he sees as needing to be fulfilled in any fully developed profession. He then assesses whether the United States meets these criteria. Toulemonde (1995) repeats this exercise for selected European countries. The results are presented in Table 6.3. It can be seen from this table that according to these nine characteristics, in no country can evaluation be said to be a fully recognized profession. However, even if evaluation cannot be formally classified as a fully fledged profession, there are various degrees of professionalization of evaluators. Toulemonde (1995) has developed a useful categorization of evaluators along a professionalization continuum:

- *Evaluation professionals*, who:
  - (a) call their work "evaluation"
  - (b) master the whole range of techniques that apply to evaluation and mix and combine these techniques as appropriate
  - (c) are specially trained and prepared for evaluation
  - (d) know the various conceptual frameworks that apply to evaluation and can swap from one to another
  - (e) devote the majority of their work time to evaluation.
- *Specialized professionals*, who meet criteria (a) to (d), but who do not devote the majority of their time to evaluation.
- *Craftsmen*, who meet criteria (a) and (b) only.
- *Amateurs*, who may call some of their activities "evaluation" but who only have a partial knowledge of evaluation theories and techniques. They have a tendency to stick to and use their own favourite approach to evaluation.

The implications of this categorization for evaluation capacity and human resource development is that governments must determine the extent to which they wish to depend on amateurs or the extent to which they wish to promote the development of craftsmen and professionals, and if so, how they should best approach this task.

Three European surveys give some findings into the supply of evaluators in this context (Toulemonde, 1995). In the first survey, conducted in 1992, one hundred interviews carried out with civil servants, academics and consultants showed that (a) European evaluation practice was growing quickly, driven by demand, and (b) the supply side of evaluation was provided by those who do evaluation mostly as a side activity (i.e., amateurs predominated). A 1993 questionnaire survey indicated a shift to craftsmen more than amateurs, with practitioners carrying out a wide variety of jobs and mastering a range of techniques. However, a small sample (220) biased in favor of well-known experts in the field and the fact that some respondents may have overestimated their skills, lends caution to this finding. A 1995 survey, with 340 responses, indicated that 39 percent of respondents devoted the major part of their professional time to evaluation, with 60 percent feeling satisfied with their capabilities to master relevant techniques.

In many ways, this question of how to support professional development is related to the issue of placement of evaluators raised above in the previous section. To what extent evaluators should specialize in evaluation and how best to apply this learning are key questions to be addressed:

TABLE 6.3
Does Evaluation Meet the Criteria for Classification as a Profession?

	United States	Netherlands	United Kingdom	Denmark
1. A need for evaluation specialists?	Yes	Yes	Yes	Yes
2. Content (knowledge and skills) unique to evaluation?	Yes	Yes	Yes	Yes
3. Preparation programs for evaluators?	Yes	Yes	Yes	No
4. Stable career opportunities in evaluation?	Yes	No	No	No
5. Certification or licence of evaluators?	No	No	No	No
6. Appropriate professional associations for evaluators?	Yes	Yes(a)	Yes(a)	Yes(a)
7. Exclusion of unqualified persons from these associations?	No	No	No	No
8. Influence of evaluators associations on preparation programs for evaluators?	No	Yes	No	No
9. Standards for the practice of evaluation?	Yes	Yes	Yes	No
(a) In all three European countries, those who wish are eligible for membership of the European Evaluation Society. The Netherlands and United Kingdom also have their own professional associations.				

Source: Worthen (1994); Toulemonde (1995)

[E]valuation capacity will mainly develop through a quantitative and qualitative shift from craftsmen towards specialised professional and from amateurs towards the upper categories. My hypothesis is that a very large proportion of evaluation work is still done by civil servants and consultants who do not deserve to be called specialized professionals. Consequently, I assume that evaluation raises excessive ambitions from the commissioner's side and that it is far from producing the added value that could be expected for the suppliers' side. My point is that there is a need to support the specialization of professionals in evaluation. Efforts should be concentrated on bridging the various gaps between different professional backgrounds. This will result in the development of activities whose legitimacy is clearly based on evaluation knowledge, evaluation skills and evaluation records, and no longer on different disciplinary or professional backgrounds. (Toulemonde,1995:53)

Conclusions

This chapter has explored some of the issues which are currently being debated and discussed with regard to the professionalization of evaluation. Various strategies for promoting an increase in the number and quality of professional evaluators have been identified at the level of: (a) ensuring appropriate curricula; (b) selecting and securing evaluators; (c) encouraging the educated consumption of evaluations; and (d) developing the profession of evaluation. Strengths and weaknesses of these strategies have been explored.

As with most of the story in this book, one of the main findings which emerges is that there is no "one right way" or quick and easy answer. Rather, it appears that a mix of strategies that have a long-term aim of professionalizing the evaluation function is appropriate. A number of elements of such an approach would appear to emerge from this review. First, it seems important to ensure, that academic curricula at a minimum include courses specifically dedicated to evaluation, and that specific dedicated evaluation programs are promoted and developed. These courses and programs should promote both methodological and interpersonal knowledge developments. Second, evaluators should be selected from a range of backgrounds and experience, rather than opting for one particular evaluator "type." Third, placing evaluators in a range of locations and using a mix of these is helpful. Specialized units, using operational managers as evaluators and utilizing outside experts and consultants are options which can be applied separately or together as appropriate to the task in hand. Fourth, ensuring that a range of in-service training and development supports are in place to enhance evaluators' competencies is important. This can include: post-graduate programs with a strong evaluation component; workshop and seminar provision on topics of interest, supported by a central agency; research into evaluation practice and procedures, in particular providing detailed case study materials giving information on such issues as context, cost, type of evaluation product, short and long-term outcomes, negative and unintended consequences of the evaluation studied; and training and development support for the commissioners and users of evaluations to create enlightened consumers. Fifth, professional evaluation associations can be a helpful means of improving the theory, practice and use of evaluations and enhance the professional development of evaluators. Sixth, there should be a policy of facilitating and encouraging a long-term trend of moving evaluators from amateur status to craftsmen to professional evaluators. And seventh, providing training and development opportunities for the commissioners and users of evaluation is important, so as to facilitate the creation of an evaluation ethos and of an educated consumer of evaluation studies.

References

Altschuld, J.W. and M. Engle (eds.). 1994. *New Directions for Program Evaluation,* 62.

Altschuld, J.W., M. Engle, C. Cullen, I. Kim, and B.R. Macce. 1994. "The 1994 Directory of Evaluation Training Programs." *New Directions for Program Evaluation,* 62: 71–93.

Bemelmans-Videc, M.L. 1992. "Institutionalizing Evaluation: International Perspectives." In J. Mayne, M.L. Bemelmans-Videc, J. Hudson, and R. Conner (eds.)., *Advancing Public Policy Evaluation: Learning from International Experiences*: 7–20. Amsterdam: Elsevier Science Publishers.

Bemelmans-Videc, M.L., B. Eriksen, and E.N. Goldenberg. 1994. "Facilitating Organizational Learning: Human Resource Management and Program Evaluation." In F.L. Leeuw, R.C. Rist, and R.C. Sonnichsen (eds.), *Can Governments Learn? Comparative Perspectives on Evaluation and Organizational Learning,* 145–87. New Brunswick, NJ: Transaction Publishers.

Boyle, R. 1995. *Towards a New Public Service*, Dublin: Institute of Public Administration.

Derlien, H.U. 1990. "Genesis and Structure of Evaluation Efforts in Comparative Perspective." In R. C. Rist (ed.), *Program Evaluation and the Management of Government: Patterns and Prospects across Eight Nations*: 147–75. New Brunswick, N.J: Transaction Publishers.

Fitzpatrick, J.L. 1994. "Alternative Models for the Structuring of Professional Preparation Programs." *New Directions for Program Evaluation,* 62: 41–50.[3]

Henry, N. 1987. "The Emergence of Public Administration as a Field of Study." In R.C. Chandler (ed.), *A Centennial History of the American Administrative State*: 37–85. New York: The Free Press.

Knox, C. and D. McAlister. 1995. "Policy Evaluation: Incorporating Users' Views." *Public Administration,* 73: 413–36.

MEANS Internal Bulletin. 1995. "The Evaluators: A Growing Network of Scandinavian Practitioners." No. 3, September, Lyon: Centre for European Evaluation Expertise.

Mertens, D.M. 1994. "Training Evaluators: Unique Skills and Knowledge." *New Directions for Program Evaluation,* 62: 17–27.

Morris, M. 1994. "The Role of Single Evaluation Courses in Evaluation Training." *New Directions for Program Evaluation,* 62: 51–59.

Narayan, D. 1993. *Participatory Evaluation.* World Bank Technical Paper No. 207. Washington, D.C.: World Bank.

News from the Community. 1995. "The Australasian Evaluation Society." *Evaluation,* 2, 1: 124–25.

Rist, R.C. 1990. "Managing of Evaluations or Managing by Evaluations: Choices and Consequences." In R.C. Rist (ed.), *Program Evaluation and the Management of Government: Patterns and Prospects Across Eight Nations*: 3–17. New Brunswick, NJ: Transaction Publishers.

Task Force on Management Improvement. 1992. *The Australian Public Service Reformed. An evaluation of a Decade of Management Reform.* Canberra: Australian Government Publishing Service.

Toulemonde, J. 1995. "The Emergence of an Evaluation Profession in European Countries: the case of Structural Policies." *Knowledge and Policy*, 8, 3:43–54.

7

Incentives, Constraints and Culture-building as Instruments for the Development of Evaluation Demand

Jacques Toulemonde

Evaluation development can be compared to the launching of an innovative product on the market. It takes an entrepreneur to design, test, produce, and finally market a new good. Thus, innovators need to be more than managers if they are to supply new goods; they must also create a demand for these goods. The same applies to the promoters of evaluation in the public sector. As an innovative practice, evaluation grows through an interactive process requiring a skilled professional community on the supply side (see Boyle, chapter 6) and a group of committed consumers on the demand side. It is not realistic to assume that evaluation fulfills an existing demand in the public sector. On the contrary, demand must be created and progressively developed at the same pace as supply, if not faster.

This chapter reviews thirteen cases in which an evaluation system has been created. Examples are taken from eight countries where evaluation has been in practice for at least ten years. The reader is referred to a short description of each example in the appendix. Most of these examples are success stories of evaluation capacity development and they are analyzed as such. It would take another chapter, or possibly another book, to explain whether these thirteen evaluation systems have proven to be fruitful or not. The following pages have a narrower scope. They simply address the question of how evaluation demand has been promoted. The main focus is on the instruments that evaluation promoters manipulated in order to create and to nurture the demand. Hereafter, these instruments are presented with the help of the metaphor of carrots, sticks and sermons (Bemelmans-Videc, Rist, and Vedung, 1998).

Creating Evaluation Demand by Incentives (Carrots)

Budgetary Incentives

Evaluation has a cost, at least for data collection, and one cannot develop an evaluation system without the necessary provision of money. Certainly the worst solution is to ask program managers to pay for evaluation by withdrawing money from their current budget. A frequent arrangement is to put a given percentage of the program's budget aside and to earmark this money for evaluation. This worked fairly well in the case of the French *Contrats de Plan Etat-Région* (see appendix: CPER).

If money is put aside, it should be carefully earmarked because evaluation is often weak compared to other public management tasks. This necessary protection is illustrated by the case of the European Structural Funds (see appendix: ECSF). All programs supported by these Funds include a special budgetary provision for "Technical Assistance" which amounts to between 2 and 5 percent of the budget. It provides resources for the setting up of monitoring information systems and for staffing a permanent program secretariat, for example, as well as for program evaluation. In theory, this organizational arrangement provides adequate funds. However, evaluation has to compete with many other expenses including, in some cases, the salary of the program secretary who plays a central role in evaluation demand. It is therefore hardly surprising that shortages of money occur when the time comes to evaluate.

Financial resources can be considered as prerequisites for the development of evaluation, but this is only one side of the coin. Channeling money for evaluation creates a clear incentive to evaluate since, according to what seems to be a universal law, civil servants like to spend public budgets (Niskanen, 1974). An illustration of this law is given by the French governmental system (see appendix: CSE) which relies heavily upon demand from Ministers. A National Fund for Evaluation Development was established with a small annual budget which helped to attract evaluation volunteers in the civil service. This partly explains why one hundred evaluation projects were spontaneously proposed by various ministers in five years. Those who see evaluation as a means to combat self-interest and increasing budgets in public administration should not forget that evaluation itself is submitted to the universal law of self-interest and the struggle for budgets. Consequently, money is an appealing incentive which can be manipulated in order to develop evaluation demand.

Career and Turnover Incentives

Some countries focus on staff rather than money. Although staff always has an equivalent in terms of budget, this way of supporting evaluation has specific advantages. A permanent team of internal evaluators can be set up and trained in a relatively short period of time. These evaluators develop skills that are finely tuned to the demand of decision makers, and usually express their conclusions in a way that is acceptable to decision makers (see Sonnichsen, chapter 2). The main drawback of internal evaluation is the risk of it being appropriated by program management, a risk which can be avoided by organizing separate careers for evaluators and program managers, as in the Canadian example (see appendix: OCG). The Canadian federal government hired about 350 persons as full-time evaluation professionals and made all of them attend a comprehensive training program in evaluation. The system allowed these professionals to move from one department to another and to build part of their careers as evaluators. Through this method, the federal government progressively created a relatively independent group of evaluation professionals. This strategy was mainly oriented towards the supply side of evaluation development but eventually had highly positive consequences on the demand side. After a few years, the "corps" of evaluation professionals acted as a lever; it helped to export the evaluation demand from one department to another.

Governments often choose to rely upon external professionals for carrying out evaluation tasks. The following is an example of a strategy aimed at organizing the professionalization of evaluation suppliers. At the initiative of the Dutch Minister of Education and Science, program evaluation was designated as one of the areas to be stimulated by a special budget. A working group was created to draw up a work plan and was eventually institutionalized in a Committee on Program Evaluation (see appendix: CPE). This Committee had a part-time secretary and met once a month over a five-year period. The CPE supported research projects, pilot evaluations, training programs, workshops and publications, and awarded an annual prize for exemplary evaluation work. Through these various instruments it played a significant role in developing one of the best professional communities of evaluators in Europe. Once again, there is no doubt that skilled academics and consultants helped to boost evaluation demand for selfish reasons (i.e.

careers and turnover). In that sense, the CPE was not only an instrument for developing the supply side of evaluation; in addition to constraints imposed by the Ministry of Finance and the Court of Audit, it also favored evaluation demand.

Carrots Create Demand, Lessons Do Not

Resources are two-faced. On the supply side, they are preconditions for the development of an evaluation capacity. On the demand side, they create incentives for the development of evaluation demand. A provision of money generates struggles for public budgets. The development of internal skills creates a group of professionals having career interests in evaluation. The development of external skills pushes evaluation through corporatist behavior. Resources are associated with the basic force which makes incentives work: self-interest.

By contrast, professional training alone has no significant impact on evaluation demand. Knowledge without interest does not work, nor does a lesson without a carrot. One can hardly imagine that decision-makers will start doing evaluations simply because they know what evaluation is. A case in point is Switzerland where the development of evaluation heavily relied on knowledge dissemination but proved to be very slow. The Swiss evaluation practice originates with the Federal Department of Justice and Police which set up a Working Group on Law Evaluation (see appendix: AGEVAL) and a special research program on the impact of federal measures. Several "state of the art" studies and pilot evaluations were commissioned. A dozen seminars, workshops and conferences were organized in the country and special evaluation training programs were proposed by universities. The research program ended after eight years and indisputably provoked a wide range of initiatives and motivation in all areas and at all governmental levels. Nevertheless, ten years after the start of the process, Swiss evaluation practice has still not reached the critical mass that would guarantee the survival of a national system. If one considers that knowledge was the main instrument that evaluation promoters could manipulate, the conclusion seems to be that this instrument is largely ineffective.

Creating Evaluation Demand by Constraint (Sticks)

Compulsory Evaluation

In some instances, political bodies have used the simplest instrument: a systematic obligation to evaluate. The European Community Structural Funds (see appendix: ECSF) provide a typical example of such compulsory evaluation. The regulations which organize these Funds include an ambitious rule of systematic evaluation which requires evaluation to be taken seriously, as the following example indicates. In the early 1990s, the Greek government, together with the European Commission, decided to evaluate a program which was partly supported by the Structural Funds. The task was contracted out to a consultant who issued his report after a few months. In the meantime, the Greek government had changed and the new minister did not want to accept and circulate the report, or pay for it. Relying upon the rule of compulsory evaluation, the European Commission threatened to interrupt the funding of the program and thereby rescued the report.

If evaluation capacity is not fully developed on the supply side, a rule of systematic compulsory evaluation is probably not workable due to a shortage of skilled professionals or to other practical impossibilities. Thus, instead of setting up unrealistic obligations, evaluation should be made compulsory in a pragmatic way. For example, the rule might apply to a small proportion of programs only, with this proportion being progressively raised in tandem with the development of evaluation skills. In the ECSF case, more than 500 programs were supposed to be evaluated at three stages of their life cycle: ex-ante, on-going and ex-post. In reality, only part of this titanic job was undertaken. European officials started to evaluate one program out of four through a reasoned process of selection.

Provided that the legal constraint is kept realistic, it furnishes evaluation promoters with an effective instrument. If the demand for evaluation is to be developed this way, however, this stick must be publicly used from time to time.

The Right to Ask Evaluation Questions

The risk with compulsory evaluation is that if they lack personal commitment, decision-makers have a tendency to steer evaluation towards calm waters and to censor critical questions (Toulemonde, 1996). This risk can be avoided by looking beyond the network of program supporters, for people wanting to attract evaluation towards sensitive areas, and by asking politically relevant questions. It might be wise to mobilize this force by granting the right to ask evaluation questions to numerous stakeholders outside the circle of program supporters (see

Mayne, Divorski, and Lemaire, chapter 1). Nevertheless, the benefits of this option have a high cost since decision makers tend to ignore the answers when they have not raised the question.

Evaluation is facilitated when the right to ask evaluation questions is given to members of powerful and well-respected institutions such as the General Accounting Office (see appendix: GAO) in the United States, which has to answer all questions asked by members of Congress. These questions run into the hundreds every year, relate to any kind of federal policy and are of all possible types (descriptive, normative, cause-and-effect). Although the GAO has a central work plan and prioritization process, each question is finally answered, after either an in-depth evaluation or a brief study. This system creates a continuous flow of evaluation demand. It relies on constraint in so far as congressional evaluative questions have to be answered.

Compulsory Access to Field Data

Only those who implement a program can provide full access to relevant field data. Their cooperation greatly helps evaluators to understand how impacts are made and how judgment criteria apply to the program in practical terms. Such cooperation can be seen as a key component of evaluation demand, which cannot be made compulsory in a simple way. An interesting example is that of the Audit Commission for England and Wales (see appendix: ACEW) which collects data from local authorities in order to operate a system of performance indicators and to undertake performance reviews. The ACEW fulfills its task by publishing detailed lists of indicators that must be measured. It also undertakes regular controls in order to ensure that the proper information systems are in place and produce reliable data. The Commission produces an annual report which synthesizes all performance indicators and provides national average values. Its legal right to open the gates for data collection gives it a deterring power, but this does not have to be used on a daily basis. On the contrary, the cooperation of local authorities is systematically sought by holding conferences and workshops and by surveying local information needs.

Compulsory Use of Evaluation Results

Is it possible to develop evaluation demand by making utilization compulsory? Once again, this is not a simple issue. A rule of compulsory utilization cannot be enforced unless very strong pressure is exerted on the civil service. Those who fail to comply with evaluation recommendations should be threatened by some form of effective sanction such as an automatic budget cut. I am not aware of any successes using this strategy and numerous counter-examples exist.

An example of failure is the Italian *Fundo per l'Investimento e l'Occupazione* (see appendix: FIO) through which the Italian State provided special support on condition that an ex-ante evaluation report demonstrate a high enough social rate of return. The rule was formally applied but the evaluation business grew at the expense of quality. Consultancy firms quickly developed evaluation branches which enjoyed a healthy turnover by systematically providing project promoters with good evaluation reports. After a few years, it was clear that evaluations hardly interacted with decision-making processes, which continued at their traditional pace. The whole evaluation activity turned out to be a meaningless ritual and the system was discontinued. This example shows the limits of the use of constraints. Decision-makers often fulfill their legal obligations without any real commitment to evaluation.

Generating Evaluation Demand through a Clever Use of Sticks

Laws and rules are meaningless on their own. At least from time to time, obligations must be enforced and power exerted; in short, the stick must be applied. Negative examples such as that of the FIO highlight the risk of establishing constraints when there is not enough power to enforce them. Smart evaluation promoters use sticks sparingly, as a deterrent (see appendix: ECSF, ACEW). They build up evaluation systems that are strongly based on power but whose superficial appearance is one of partnership and discussion.

The Dutch system of Reconsideration of Public Expenditures (see appendix: RPE) is an example of a smart use of sticks as instruments of evaluation development. The annual rounds of the RPE include from ten to fifteen evaluation studies which are authoritatively agreed through full cabinet decisions. Each evaluation is the responsibility of a specially appointed interdepartmental working group. The latter receive central steering and secretarial assistance from the Ministry of Finance. They are not required to speak with a single voice and the final report may include opposing points of view. Evaluations are issued in connection with the budgetary process and must include an alternative program proposing a 20 percent saving in the budget. During the first decade of the RPE, about one third of the evaluation results were directly used to reduce budgets. No clear pattern has been found to explain this successful utilization. It did not result from an especially high quality of the evaluation reports, nor from an especially low level of resistance by bureaucrats (Van Nisper tot Pannerden, 1994). The Dutch system uses many constraints such as centrally decided evaluation plans and systematic proposals of budget cuts. Nevertheless, these constraints are applied in a flexible way and stakeholders are involved in the evaluation process with some degree of freedom. This smart use of sticks has created a sustained evaluation activity, of which a reasonable proportion has proved to be useful.

Mixing Carrots and Sticks:
An Individualistic Model of Evaluation Demand

This section proposes a model explaining how incentives and constraints deserve to be applied together. The reasoning considered here is deliberately individualistic. It explains evaluation demand from the standpoint of a single decision-maker who is assumed to behave in accordance with the balance of positive and negative consequences of his/her choice. The subject of the reasoning is any person who has to decide upon the evaluation of a program, to ask an evaluative question, to open a door for data collection or to accept the conclusion of a report. The model applies to someone who is practically capable of supporting or blocking an evaluation at any one of its stages. The reasoning is analyzed with the help of a "decision tree" with a trunk and six branches, as shown in diagram 7.1:

Decision to Evaluate ("Yes" or "No")

The trunk of the tree consists of the decision to launch or to support an evaluation. It has two main branches: "yes" and "no." The "yes" branch always has a direct cost which occurs with the simple fact that the decision is made to undertake evaluation , whatever the conclusion of the report. An example of direct costs is the time and money spent in the evaluation process. By contrast, the "no" branch normally involves no direct cost or any other indirect consequence. The "yes" branch is always a problematic compound of assumed costs and benefits, while the "no" branch is appealing by its simple neutrality.

In many cases, evaluation demand has been developed by manipulating the attractiveness of both branches. The principle is to put car-

Diagram 7.1
The Evaluation Decision Tree

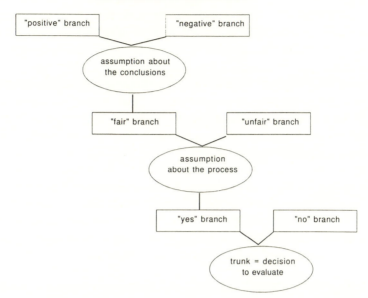

rots on the "yes" branch and sticks on the "no" branch. An example is given by the system of the French *Contrats de Plan Etat-Région* (State-Region Joint Plans, see appendix: CPER). In order to encourage regional authorities to evaluate, the promoters of the system reduced the direct cost of evaluation in several ways. First, the national government decided to retain 0.06 percent from its financial commitments within the CPER and to earmark this money for evaluation. It was proposed that the regions do the same from their side. The 0.06percent levy acted as a powerful incentive while removing the cost barrier to evaluation demand. The system then created another incentive and removed another barrier by proposing that State-Region evaluation committees keep control over the publication of evaluation reports. This allowed regional authorities to protect themselves against the risk of losing control over strategic information. Only after this facility was given did the most reluctant regions agree to play the evaluation game.

In the Australian case, the decision was made to put some sticks on the "no" branch. This has been done by requiring Portfolios (Departments) to issue Evaluation Plans. The plans are negotiated with the Department of Finance. This creates a cost of not doing evaluation, namely a need to spend time and energy in explaining why a program should not be submitted to evaluation.

Assumption About the Evaluation Process ("Fair" or "Unfair")

If the "yes" branch is chosen, the next two branches relate to the fairness of the evaluation process. A "fair" process is likely to strengthen the network of people who have stakes in the program, making the decision to evaluate more attractive. By contrast, doubts as to the fairness of evaluation make the whole game unpredictable. The conclusion of an "unfair" evaluation depends on the powers and tactical skills of the various players, something which is extremely difficult to foresee. In this case, the only reasonable behavior is to resist, either actively or passively, and to opt for the "no" branch of the decision tree, no matter how many incentives or constraints apply to its other branches. Fairness is a particularly sensitive issue since evaluators have to make explicit value judgments without being equipped with ready-to-use criteria and benchmarks. It can seldom be taken for granted, especially in the first years of the development of evaluation when deontological rules, quality standards and professionalization are not fully established. This explains why confidence is a basic ingredient of evaluation demand.

From this standpoint, an interesting arrangement is that of the French *Conseil Scientifique de l'Evaluation* (see appendix: CSE). The ministers who initiate evaluation projects must submit their draft terms of reference to an ex-ante quality assessment. Up to now, the CSE has assessed twenty-eight evaluation projects. It has at times rejected individual evaluative questions or even rejected complete evaluation projects which partly overlooked the views of various stakeholders or were not of an evaluative nature. The CSE also carries out ex-post quality control at the final report stage. During its six years in operation, it has established the "rules of the game" that ensure a fair evaluation process, that is, involve key stakeholders in an evaluation group, present intermediary reports to the evaluation group, separate fact finding and analysis activities by consultants from judgment making by the evaluation group, and so forth. The CSE is composed of eleven members, half of them being top civil servants and the other half well-respected academics. Its role as guarantor partly explains why numerous evaluation demands have appeared within a system that relies solely upon volunteers.

The example of the Audit Commission for England and Wales (see appendix: ACEW) illustrates another way of securing fairness which is more informal and pragmatic. The Commission was created by the government in order to ensure that local authorities made proper arrangements for achieving economy, efficiency and effectiveness in the management of their resources. Since the context was one of reducing the autonomy of local authorities, the ACEW's activities risked being seen as unfair. Nevertheless, it managed to create confidence in evaluation by developing close cooperation with those under evaluation and by including among its members people with past and present connections with local authorities. An important part of its success derives from its choice of evaluation topics relevant to the needs of local authorities. Evaluation teams often comprise top managers or other senior people nominated from local authorities.

These two examples show how fairness can be secured either by a compulsory system of quality assessment (stick), or by a highly participative approach to evaluation (carrot).

Prediction About the Evaluation Conclusions (Positive or Negative)

If the evaluation process can be considered as "fair" and if the "yes" branch is chosen, the highest branches of the decision tree relate to the evaluation report itself: will it shed a good or a bad light on the program? Decision makers always make their own intuitive assessment of the program under evaluation, which shapes their opinion on whether a fair report will judge the program favorably or not. They will strongly anticipate a favorable report if they personally support the program, while opponents of the program will expect criticism.

The ultimate consequences of the evaluation for an individual stakeholder depend on whether or not the report is in line with his/her expectations. A favorable report leads to "positive" consequences for a program supporter as well as a critical report does for a program opponent. Since almost all people involved with evaluation demand have stakes in the program, some of them will inevitably fear negative consequences while others will expect positive ones. Only "pure" neutral administrators, evenly agreeing to kill bad programs and continue good ones, would always feel that evaluation has "positive" consequences. The problem with ultimate consequences is that they can hardly be manipulated. Critical reports and/or negative consequences inherently belong to the evaluation game and there is no point in introducing a bias in favor of complacent evaluation. Evaluation promoters must accept a kind of "law of symmetry" which states that some programs are good and others not, that some programs are judged as good by evaluators and other not, and that evaluation satisfies some stakeholders and not others. When a country tends to link evaluation and budgetary allocation (e.g., Australia or the Netherlands), the law of symmetry also applies so that good programs are likely to have their budget increased and bad programs are threatened by budget cuts. Structured feed-back mechanisms make the "positive" branch more attractive and the "negative" one more frightening. If such mechanisms apply to a large number of evaluations, they are likely to generate a greater number of both supporters and opponents of evaluation, in a symmetric way. That is why linking budgeting and evaluation is a very difficult task (see Gray, Jenkins, and Segsworth, 1993, and Bastoe, chapter 4).

In the search for new instruments to manipulate evaluation demand, one can link budgeting and evaluation in an asymmetrical way. This idea emerged in Colombia when all departments were submitted to systematic budget cuts. The national planning agency suggested that a few programs could escape the budget cuts provided they demonstrate good achievements through evaluation. I suggested a similar idea in the framework of a recent evaluation in Belgium (European Commission, 1995). A 1,500 Million ECU program (USD 1,900 million) was under evaluation and the funding authorities planned to allocate a complementary budget amounting to 5 percent of the program. The evaluation was designed to influence the allocation of this additional budget. In the Colombian case, as in the Belgian one, the evaluation itself does not generate a risk of budgetary cuts. The process is turned into a positive sum game with the aim of creating a cooperative attitude among stakeholders towards evaluation.

Decentralization (see Sonnichsen, chapter 2) is another strategy that can be applied to ensure that the ultimate consequences of evaluation are always seen as "positive," and to sustain evaluation demand. It enables decision-makers to master all the consequences of an evaluation report, whether their program is eventually judged as good or bad. Decentralized evaluation looks like self-evaluation or like what Fetterman (1994) proposes under the label of "empowerment evaluation." It is a powerful instrument of evaluation development that should not be forgotten. Some interesting features of the strategy exist in the evaluation system of the Job Training Partnership Act (see appendix: JTPA) in the USA. This system included a rule of compulsory evaluation but the practice was left entirely to the initiative of the States which had to set up the organizational arrangements. No guidelines were issued at Federal level. An attempt to undertake a large national evaluation project met with a considerable amount of political resistance. By contrast, decentralized projects appeared to grow successfully, at least in quantity. In less than ten years, nearly 190 evaluation studies were carried out. State and local evaluators came together in a network which initiated training workshops. The network promoters published several guidelines, as well as "Evaluation Forum," a special journal whose title neatly illustrates the decentralized way of developing evaluation.

In Search of the Proper Mix of Constraints and Incentives

It is now possible to summarize how incentives and constraints can apply to the various branches of the decision tree discussed above. The following recipes have been tried and proven:

- obligation to establish an evaluation work plan: a stick that makes the "no" branch more difficult
- provision of money earmarked for evaluation: a carrot that makes the "yes" branch more attractive
- right to keep evaluation information under control: a carrot that makes the "yes" branch more attractive;
- systematic quality assessment: a stick that makes the "unfair" branch more unlikely;
- systematic consultation and involvement of stakeholders: a carrot that makes the "fair" branch more likely;
- decentralization: a carrot that helps decision makers to assume "positive" consequences.

This list of recipes shows that constraints and incentives can be mixed and applied to all factors of evaluation demand. The art of combining the various instruments is illustrated by two French examples below.

The French governmental evaluation system (see appendix: CSE) relies heavily upon demand from Ministers. This demand has been successfully manipulated by means of two instruments: a carrot on the "yes" branch (National Fund for the Development of Evaluation) and a guarantee of "fair" evaluation (Scientific Council of Evaluation). Nevertheless, the system has not proved to be very convincing and after six years in operation its future is far from certain. Its weaknesses appear when one looks at the nature of the evaluations which have been undertaken to date. The first evaluation dealt with the effects of computers in the civil service, a topic hardly likely to disrupt the political agenda, and was followed by many other subjects of equally minor importance. The financial carrot and the guarantee of fairness have successfully created a demand for evaluation. However, these instruments have not been powerful enough to overcome the reluctance of the bureaucracy to address politically sensitive issues, or the collective avoidance of conflicts which prevail in some political circles. The lesson from this example is that a certain degree of constraint needs to be applied; at least a few sticks should be included in the mix of instruments.

The evaluation system of the Rhône-Alpes region (see appendix: RAR) has achieved a better balance of sticks and carrots. It was born in 1990 when the Regional Council (legislative branch) obliged the regional executive to set up an evaluation system. This potentially conflicting origin is not, however, visible in the features of a system which has turned out to be highly participative. The executive branch produces annual evaluation work plans, each of which covers about four major regional programs. Program managers are closely involved in the framing of the evaluation questions. Once decided, the evaluation process is open to all major political leaders, including opponents in the regional council, and to representatives of the relevant lobbies. Up to fifty stakeholders gather in an evaluation group which holds four or five meetings during the evaluation process. These meetings are, moreover, surprisingly well attended. A scientific committee is responsible for validating the methodological quality and ensuring the fairness of regional evaluations. Sticks are not absent from the system which, all in all, runs fairly smoothly. Recently, the Regional Council requested the executive to publicly respond to the conclusions of an evaluation. The evaluation system had proved capable of creating a collective interest and a spirit of confidence in the evaluation work. It was easily renewed after the first three years in operation.

As a first conclusion to this study, it can be said that evaluation demand develops faster when incentives and constraints are mixed and applied to all branches of the decision tree. Nevertheless, one must go further than this first conclusion. If some clever promoters were capable of manipulating all relevant carrots and sticks, would this suffice to overcome all political and bureaucratic resistance to evaluation? The answer is clearly no.

There will always be instances where people involved with evaluation demand predict dramatically "negative" consequences of evaluation, like the death of their program, the destruction of their legitimacy or even the loss of their jobs. If an evaluation function is anchored in another part of the institutional setting rather than the program, such a risky evaluation can be effectively supported (see Mayne, Divorski, and Lemaire, chapter 1). Nevertheless, if such drastic threats hang from the top branches of the decision tree, all the other branches will simply be forgotten by those who fear evaluation, no matter what incentives and constraints they offer. From their point of view, incentives will simply be neglected and constraints will systematically be resisted or turned around. This explains why even the best mix of carrots and sticks will never eradicate the pockets of resistance to evaluation.

Evaluation Demand and Culture-building (Sermon)

Let us imagine why a decision maker might opt for evaluation when this dramatically contradicts his/her self-interest, and let us call this reason "goodwill." Is there any instrument which can be manipulated in order to develop this goodwill? Such an instrument does indeed exist: it is the building of an evaluation culture. Once this culture is well established, evaluation is deeply rooted in the administrative values, is seen as an undisputed duty and becomes one of the fundamentals of the governing system. The culture provides the collective pressure that makes decision-makers overcome their reluctance, even when evaluation deeply contradicts their self-interest.

Establishing an evaluation culture requires more than an intense and sustained communication effort. Its success depends less on the content of the message or the quality of communication techniques than on how well-respected the messengers are and how many colleagues have already been convinced. In a certain sense, the process of developing an evaluation culture resembles that of preaching faith: the "sermon" seems to be the relevant instrument. In the context of public administration, sermons take the form of conferences, workshops, training courses, newsletters and journals. They make extensive use of demonstration projects, success stories, visits to good practitioners, prizes, and awards. Those who listen to the sermon should be convinced that they belong to a community of people who trust that evaluation is part of sound public management. Civil servants should become proud of their job when they evaluate. The evaluation culture of a decision-maker relies very much upon the social pressure exerted by his/her colleagues. In a certain sense, one should apply the same type of instrument in building an evaluation culture as in launching a new management fashion.

At the end of this review of thirteen international experiences, the lesson which emerges is that all instruments should be applied together: incentives, constraints, and culture building. In order to create an evaluation demand, one must use carrots, sticks and sermons altogether. This conclusion is well illustrated by the case of Australia (see appendix: APS) which boosted evaluation practice most effectively through a clever mix of all three. Major Australian programs are required to be evaluated every three to five years in the framework of rolling annual "Portfolio Evaluation Plans" (sticks). The Department of Finance supplies consultancy services and staff support to evaluation demanders (carrots). Many civil servants belong to evaluation networks and since 1991 more than 2500 officials have attended one-day evaluation workshops. An evaluation register is published and now covers 500 reports (sermons). An observer of Australian practice considers that evaluation contributes to job satisfaction in the civil service by increasing the belief that programs can be improved (Mackay, 1993). A series of surveys carried out between 1991 and 1994 shows that out of the new policy proposals, up to 77 percent (1994–95) were influenced by evaluations. While clever evaluation promoters use carrots and sticks at all branches of the evaluation decision tree, they also acknowledge that nothing except sermons can overcome human resistance in the most difficult cases.

Such an all-embracing and general conclusion might not be of much help for those who start building an evaluation system and have to choose the first stone. Very often at this early stage many instruments are simply not available. Can we start building an evaluation system if constraint is unthinkable? Can we keep developing evaluation demand if there is a shortage of carrots? When looking at the various experiences under review, it seems that some success can be obtained when evaluation promoters are limited in their capacity to manipulate the various instruments. Their weaknesses simply result in a slower development of evaluation demand. This happened in the Swiss example (see appendix: AGEVAL). The Swiss constitutional setting involves so many checks and balances that evaluation promoters were unable to manipulate constraints and incentives. Their major instrument was the dissemination of evaluation knowledge and they also tried to build an evaluation culture. Their efforts led to obvious—albeit very slow—progress in evaluation practice but they did not fully achieve the setting up of a Swiss evaluation system.

Contrasting the Australian and Swiss examples, one can conclude that it is possible to develop a large and sustainable evaluation capacity on the demand side in less than ten years, provided that all instruments are available for manipulation. Progress will be slower if some instruments are missing.

Appendix: Thirteen Experiences of Institutionalization

ACEW—Audit Commission for England and Wales

The Audit Commission for England and Wales was established in 1982 as an independent body of twenty members. In July 1991, the British government asked the Commission to operate a system of performance indicators and to undertake performance reviews in order to ensure that local authorities make proper arrangements for achieving economy, efficiency and effectiveness in the management of their resources. Dozens of studies are undertaken every year in policy fields related to the delivery of local services. The Commission produces an annual report which displays all performance data and provides national average values.

More details in : Henkel M. 1996. "Evaluative Institutions in England and Wales: Weak Versions of Intergovernmental Evaluation" in O. Rieper and J. Toulemonde (ed.), *The Politics and Practice of Intergovernmental Evaluation.* New Brunswick: Transaction Publishers.

AGEVAL—Groupe de travail "Evaluation législative"

In 1987, the Swiss Federal Department of Justice and Police set up a Working Group on Law Evaluation (AGEVAL). The Group included members of both the executive and legislative branches at federal level, representatives of the cantons, and high-level academics. From 1987 to 1991 the AGEVAL held twelve meetings. The same Federal Department of Justice and Police also initiated a research program on the impact of federal measures (PNR 27) which was launched in 1987 by the Federal Council with a CHF 5 million (USD 4 million) budget over seven years. This research program applied to all policy fields, not only those of Justice and Police. After almost ten years, no evaluation system formally exists in Switzerland. Swiss evaluation practice can be estimated at around ten to twenty reports per year.

More details in : Bussmann W. 1995. "Evaluation and Grassroots Politics: The Case of Switzerland." *Knowledge and Policy* 8, 3, 85–98.

APS—Australian Public Service

The Australian Public Service (APS) evaluation system was set up by the federal executive in 1988. This regime applies to all federal portfolios (ministries). It is strongly promoted by the Department of Finance. Evaluation practice amounts to ten to twenty reports a year.

More details in: Mackay K. 1993. "Federal initiatives: the evolution of evaluation in the commonwealth government" in *Evaluation: Improving Program Performance and Decision Making.* Parkes ACT Australia: Department of Finance, 9–17 and in: Sedgwick, S.T. 1992. "Encouraging Evaluation in the Australian Budget Sector" in J. Mayne et al. (ed.), *Advancing Public Policy Evaluation: Learning from International Experiences.* Amsterdam: Elsevier Science Publishers, 37–48.

CPE—Committee on Program Evaluation

In 1984, the Dutch Minister of Education and Science issued a policy statement on the "behavioral and social sciences". With the support of the Parliament, a working group was institutionalized in a Committee on Program Evaluation (CPE). This Committee was assigned a budget of NLG 5.7 million (USD 3.4 million) for the period 1986–1991. It had a part-time secretary and met once a month. The CPE supported research projects, pilot evaluations, training programs, workshops and publications. It did not lead to a formal evaluation system but made a significant contribution to the development of the Dutch evaluation capacity (see RPE).

More details in: Hofstee W.K.B. and Laros J.A. 1989. "Stimulating Program Evaluation: the Dutch Experience." *Impact assessment bulletin*, 7, 2–3, 15–25.

CPER—Contrats de Plan Etat-Région

The French State-Region joint plans (CPERs) are agreed every five years through a negotiation process involving the French Government and each of the twenty-six regional governments. A CPER consists of a plan that harmonizes major public programs funded by both levels of government in almost all policy fields. Although several rounds of

CPERs have already taken place, the first evaluation system was set up in 1993. In each region, national and regional authorities establish an evaluation work plan which is implemented in partnership. A national scientific committee is in charge of an ex-ante assessment of the quality of evaluations. In the framework of this system, evaluation practice amounts to about fifty reports per year.

(This experience has not yet been reported in the scientific literature.)

CSE—Conseil Scientifique de l'Evaluation

In 1990 the French national executive established an evaluation system which provides for several large evaluations per year, each of them involving several ministers. Evaluation projects are initiated by ministers on a voluntary basis in almost all policy fields. The ministers who initiate these projects must submit their draft terms of reference to an ex-ante quality assessment by a Scientific Council of Evaluation (CSE). Once agreed, the evaluation projects benefit from the support of a National Fund for Evaluation Development which amounts to FRF 4 million per year (USD 0.8 million). The CSE also carries out ex-post quality control at the final report stage. In the framework of this system, evaluation practice amounts to about five reports per year.

More details in: Nioche, J.P. 1992. "Institutionalizing Evaluations in France: Skating on Thin Ice" in J. Mayne et al. (ed.), *Advancing Public Policy Evaluation: Learning from International Experiences.* Amsterdam: Elsevier Science Publishers, 23–36 and in: Duran P., Monnier E., and Smith A. 1995. "Evaluation "à la française": towards a new relationship between social science and public action. *Evaluation: the International Journal of Theory, Research and Practice*, 1, 1, 45–63.

ECSF—European Community Structural Funds

The European Community Structural Funds (ECSF) are mainly targeted at regions whose development is lagging behind. They cover a wide range of policy fields from basic infrastructure to human resource development. The funds are spent through a system of joint programming and joint financing which involves the European Commission, the Member States and the relevant regional authorities. Since 1988, the regulations of Structural Funds include an ambitious rule of systematic evaluation. In the framework of this system, evaluation practice amounts to 100–200 reports per year.

More details in : Toulemonde J. 1995. "The Emergence of an Evaluation Profession in Europe" *Knowledge and Policy*, 8, 3, 43–54.

FIO—Fundo per l'Investimento e l'Occupazione

In the early 1980s the Italian government set up the FIO (*Fundo per l"Investimento e l'Occupazione*—Investment and Employment Fund) aimed at rationalizing the allocation of budgetary funds to ministries and local authorities in a wide range of policy fields. The system included a rule of compulsory ex-ante evaluation using cost-benefit analysis. The ministry of finance applied the rule in a systematic way and issued detailed guidelines. Evaluation practice expanded to hundreds of evaluations per year. The system was discontinued at the end of the 1980s.

More details in : Pennisi G., Petterlini E. 1987 *Spesa pubblica e bisogno di inefficienza* Bologna: Il Mulino.

GAO—General Accounting Office

The General Accounting Office depends on the United States Congress. Approximately 80 percent of its work originates from congressional requests. It has answered evaluation demands since the late 1960s in all policy fields and its evaluation practice amounts to about 200 reports per year.

More details in: Rist R. 1992. "Program evaluation in the U.S. General Accounting Office: reflections on question formulation and utilization" in J. Mayne et al. (ed.) *Advancing Public Policy Evaluation: Learning from International Experiences*. Amsterdam: Elsevier Science Publishers, 149–56.

JTPA—Job Training Partnership Act

The Job Training Partnership Act (JTPA) was adopted by the Congress of the USA in 1982. The JTPA was implemented by the states, in association with local authorities and private sector organizations. Federal funding was divided up between the states on the basis of needs indicators. As regards the local programs, the role of agents at the federal level was limited to defining targets and performance standards, and to participating in monitoring and evaluation. In the framework of this system, evaluation practice amounted to about twenty reports per year.

More details in: Upjohn Institute for Employment Research. 1990. *Evaluating Social Programs at State and Local Level.* Kalamazoo.

OCG—Office of the Comptroller General

Canada institutionalized an evaluation system at the federal level of government in 1977. The regime was boosted by a series of governmental regulations. It was led by a fifteen-member professional unit in the Office of the Comptroller General (OCG). Evaluation soon became common practice in the forty-three major departments and agencies and 80–100 evaluations were completed each year.

More details in: Leclerc G. 1992. "Institutionalizing Evaluation in Canada" in J. Mayne et al. (ed.) *Advancing Public Policy Evaluation: Learning from International Experiences.* Amsterdam: Elsevier Science Publishers, 49–58.

RAR—Région Rhône-Alpes

The Rhône-Alpes Region (RAR) in France established an evaluation system in 1990 at the request of the Regional Council (legislative branch). The executive branch produces a rolling evaluation work plan which covers all fields of regional policies. Evaluations are undertaken by the executive with significant involvement by the members of the Council. A regional scientific committee acts as a guarantor of quality. Regional evaluation practice amounts to four reports per year.

(This experience has not yet been reported in the scientific literature)

RPE—Reconsideration of Public Expenditures

The Reconsideration of Public Expenditures was set up in 1981 when the Dutch government set up a procedure of systematic reviews aimed at cutting-back public expenditure in all policy fields. The RPE is organized in annual rounds. Each round includes from ten to fifteen evaluation studies which are agreed through full cabinet decisions. Evaluation studies are issued in connection with the budgetary process.

More details in: Bemelmans-Videc, M.L. 1989. "Dutch experience in the utilization of evaluation research: the procedure of reconsideration." *Knowledge in Society,* 2, 4, 31–48. And for Dutch speakers in van Nisper tot Pannerden F. 1994. *Het dossier Heroverweging.* Delft.

References

Bemelmans-Videc M.L., Rist R.C., and Vedung E. (eds.). 1998. *Carrots, Sticks and Sermons: Policy instruments and their Evaluation.* New Brunswick, NJ: Transaction Publishers.

Derlien H.U. 1990. "Genesis and Structure of Evaluation Efforts in Comparative Perspective." In Rist R.C. (ed.), *Program evaluation and the management of government: patterns and prospects across eight nations.* New Brunswick, NJ: Transaction Publishers.

European Commission. 1995. "Applying the Multi-criteria Method to the Evaluation of Structural Programmes." *MEANS Handbook* 4. Brussels: European Commission—DG XVI.

Fetterman D.M. 1994. "Empowerment evaluation." *Evaluation Practice*, 15, 1–15.

Gray A., Jenkins B., and Segsworth B. 1993. *Budgeting, Auditing and Evaluation: Functions and Integration in Seven Governments.* New Brunswick, NJ: Transaction Publishers.

Niskanen W.J. 1974. *Bureaucracy and Representative Government.* Chicago: Aldine Publishing Company.

Toulemonde J. 1996. "Europe and the Member States: Cooperating and Competing on Evaluation Grounds." In Rieper O. and Toulemonde J. (eds.), *Politics and Practice of Intergovernmental Evaluation.* New Brunswick, NJ: Transaction Publishers.

Part 4

Institutionalizing Evaluation—
The Lessons Learnt

8

Evaluation Capacity Development in Developing Countries: Applying the Lessons from Experience

R. Pablo Guerrero

Introduction

Earlier chapters have discussed best practices in institutionalizing a public sector evaluation function in industrial countries. The reasons that led to the establishment of evaluation as a tool of governance and to evaluation capacity building in these countries are also at the root of initiatives in developing countries. The rationale underlying the role of evaluation in public sector reform in developing countries is well articulated by Wiesner (1993, 1997). In a nutshell, Wiesner has observed that in many developing countries, including his native Colombia, in spite of sound macroeconomic management, the growth rate of the economy has stagnated. A main cause has been the constraining influence of a large and inefficient public sector. He attributes this public sector inefficiency in great measure to lack of competition in the delivery of public services. Government agencies behave as monopolies, not subject to real market tests, to a large extent unaccountable, and captured by rent seeking special interests. While in the private sector, competition and prices largely determine whether a business thrives or goes bust, public sector service delivery by government agencies has not been contested. Wiesner argues that transparent public sector evaluations provide the "market" signals which would effectively show tax payers and civil society at large whether the public sector is delivering services efficiently and effectively.

In essence, public sector evaluations of major government programs provide signals which proxy those which make the market function. In discussing the role of evaluation, Havens (1992) has articulated a complementary point: "the more that we [public administrators] know about how our programs are functioning, effects they are having, and at what cost, the more likely we are to search out ways of making them more efficient and more effective. To a substantial degree, this knowledge is the public-sector manager's surrogate for the profit-and-loss statement of the business sector."

The World Bank (1994) sees public sector evaluation as a necessary component of the increasing number of public sector reform programs and good governance initiatives it's supporting throughout developing countries. Stiglitz (1989, 1994) provides a more theoretical basis for public sector evaluation. In analyzing the role of the state, Stiglitz has shown the unique role information asymmetry plays in public failure, affecting negatively the public sector role in economic management, and by implication in economic development. Information asymmetry refers to the fact that economic agents do not all have access to the same information and therefore make decisions based on imperfect knowledge leading to suboptimal resource allocation. Arguably, to the extent that public sector evaluations produce valuable and accessible information about the management of public resources, their availability reduces information asymmetry among economic agents and, other things equal, impact positively on the welfare enhancing role of the state. Bates (1995) would argue that public sector evaluation is a non-market solution or institution which compensates for market failures. There is ample evidence based, for example, on World Bank sponsored evaluations of public sector projects and programs, that indeed public sector evaluations can lead to improved public sector resource allocation over time. This type of evidence is at the root of the increasing interest in evaluation capacity development in developing countries today.

This chapter concerns the practical aspects of evaluation capacity development in developing countries. It seeks to illustrate how selected developing countries have approached the institutionalization of evaluation in government. The demand and supply framework for evaluation capacity building, and the key issues addressed in earlier chapters, provide the road map. This chapter proposes to explore the context and the key issues with respect to emerging experience in three developing countries: Colombia, China, and Indonesia. These are countries where The World Bank has been supporting government evaluation efforts.

Experience in industrial countries shows that each country has unique institutional characteristics which make generalizations difficult, inadvisable, or risky. Derlien (1990) has shown that there are as many forms of government and public sector organization in industrial countries as there are types of evaluation systems. Yet, within existing systems, there are evaluation practices worth examining and perhaps emulating or adapting in developing countries. It is not coincidence that when developing country governments have decided to move forward with institutionalizing an evaluation function, one of their first priorities has been to learn as much as possible about the development of the evaluation function in industrial countries and how it works today.

For reference, and to better understand the context of the cases discussed, it is important to note that the three subject countries have very different forms of government organization which affect the institutionalization of evaluation capacity. Colombia has a multiparty democratic system of government with a president, congress and senate elected by direct universal suffrage. China is governed by a single party system, with a national people's congress elected by citizens, which in turn selects a president and premier. Indonesia is a presidential republic with a house of representatives and a people's consultative assembly, which includes the members of the house, elected by universal suffrage. As will be discussed below, each has pursued the institutionalization of a public sector evaluation function in different ways.

For ease of presentation, the discussion of the country cases follows three major streams. The first addresses the demand for evaluation, and covers the issues of leadership, incentives, and the institutional set up. The second addresses issues of organization of the evaluation function and actionable steps. The third, addresses supply issues—including evaluation capacity, that is, staffing and skills, financial resources, and methods. The perspectives afforded by the three cases provide a basis for approaching institutionalization of evaluation in other countries. Table 8.1 summarizes where these countries stand with respect to institutionalizing evaluation.

Demand Considerations

Experience shows that without effective demand, that is, demand based on real pressures on governments, any effort to institutionalize a public sector evaluation function will quickly lead to disinterest and evaporation. What are the circumstances that led these three countries

TABLE 8.1
Evaluation Capacity Development and Institutionalization
Key Issues addressed in Colombia, China, and Indonesia

Issue	Colombia	China	Indonesia
Anchoring the Evaluation Regime	Constitution mandates the Executive to take lead	State Council draft resolution calls on the Central Executive Agencies to take lead	Responsibility rests with the Executive through a Ministerial decree
Positioning the Evaluation Functions	Centralized in the National Planning Department (NPD). Key line agencies provide inputs.	Decentralized to key central agencies.	Centralized in the National Development Planning Agency (BAPPENAS). Line agencies provide inputs.
Evaluation Coverage	Public policy and major public sector programs	Public sector projects	Development policies, plans, programs, and projects
Linking Evaluation with other Public Sector Functions	NPD plays a key role in policy and strategy formulation and budget allocation and monitoring.	No formal links have been established. State Planning Commission involved in public resources allocation and monitoring	BAPPENAS to link evaluation to the annual budget allocation process.
Using Evaluation in Decision-Making	Monitoring and evaluation information to flow to line agency heads and the NPD	Monitoring and evaluation information to inform central agency management	Monitoring and evaluation information to flow through line agency management to BAPPENAS.
Professionalizing the Evaluation Function	Evaluation is a trans-discipline, cutting across specific professional skills	Evaluation is seen primarily as applied socio-economic analysis.	Evaluation is not seen as a separate profession, but a complementary discipline.
Fostering demand for Evaluation	Evaluation to be mainstreamed in agencies' budgets	Evaluation mainstreamed in central agencies' budgets	Evaluation mainstreamed in agencies' budgets

to move forward on evaluation and what were the first steps? First, all these countries have been facing increasingly hard resource constraints to finance ever more demanding development plans. Population growth and people's expectations about better life standards, fed in part by the world-wide information revolution, have put pressure on governments to deliver more and higher quality public services. Public sector budgets, whether internally or externally financed, have strained to keep pace with public expenditure needs. Government political promises and commitments have additionally fueled pressures to improve public sector efficiency in resource allocation. Second, the implementation of development policies, plans and programs, particularly those internally financed, has not always met anticipated objectives. Many expensive public sector programs, including some externally financed, have failed to fully meet their objectives efficiently, and have hence generated disappointment and discontent, and pressures on public agencies to improve the use of public resources. Third, poor performance, and the realization that more productive use of resources can be achieved, has led for calls by civil society and organized political opposition to call for strengthened government accountability for the use of public funds, and more generally for improvements in governance.

In all three countries, the demand for evaluation has originated in one or more of the above circumstances. By deciding to move forward with institutionalizing public sector evaluation functions, these governments have accepted that evaluation is an essential institution of good governance. Yet, in all three cases, while demand has been a necessary condition for making the decision to start evaluation capacity development programs, leadership and vision to enact action on evaluation capacity has been the linchpin. In the three countries, leadership has been exercised in vastly different ways.

In Colombia, in 1991, the government of President Cesar Gaviria commissioned a high level study to assess how Colombia should institutionalize an evaluation function. The government had been exposed to an external evaluation of investments in the key power sector showing that Colombia could have improved substantially the outcome and services of multi-billion-dollar investments in the sector. The high-level study was commissioned to study the feasibility of introducing evaluation to cover major public sector expenditures. While doing the study, the government quickly recognized that in order to institutionalize the function would require political consensus bridging the interests of all concerned parties. To do so, the government commissioned five independent evaluations of large controversial public sector programs. These programs covered a period which transcended various political regimes, and included a hydroelectric, an urban rapid transit, a papermill, a community welfare, and an international communications project (DNP, 1992). The aim of the evaluations was to enrich the dialog among the various interest groups by providing them with specific evaluation results comparing what had been achieved with what could have been done, had those evaluations been available earlier in the decision making processes. The results of these evaluations were discussed in a high-level conference where past and present government decisions makers, international experts, and political interest groups participated. The conclusion of the conference led to a recommendation that the Colombian constitution, which was being re-drafted at the time, should include an article making public sector evaluation mandatory. Thus, through leadership, stakeholder involvement, and opportunism, a legal foundation for evaluation was established in Colombia.

In China, the early steps were taken by the country's Auditor General. The Auditor General had, through his extensive relationships with auditors in industrial countries, and through formal contacts such as with the International Organization of Supreme Audit Institutions, become aware of and interested in performance auditing and program evaluation. While initially the Auditor General was particularly interested in starting by enhancing the State Audit Administration evaluation capabilities, a State Council decision to involve other key ministries was made. This broadened the diagnosis of the institutional framework on which to develop an evaluation system. In 1992, the Auditor General, the Ministry of Finance, the State Planning Commission, and other key central agencies, decided to move forward with an institutional study which would develop alternative proposals for recommendation to the State Council. Some of the specifics of the process are well detailed in Hong and Rist (1997). But, the salient feature of the approach followed by China was that the Ministry of Finance, as the public agency spearheading the effort, realized that progress was going to be made if all relevant major public agencies were part of the process. Early on, the Ministry of Finance organized a steering committee with representatives of the major public agencies. This was the first time that many of these senior Chinese officials had ever met or worked together on any initiative. The steering group, with support from national and international experts, drafted a proposal with various alternatives for an evaluation system (Khan 1994). The proposals were later discussed and an approach agreed in principle at a high level ministerial conference. While formal approval for the preferred proposal is pending in the State Council, in 1995, tacit approval was given to the State Planning Commission to draft regulations governing evaluation in public sector agencies. Various key central agencies began to institutionalize evaluation capabilities within their own organizations. Today, more than ten major public agencies have set up evaluation offices and work programs. Prior to the Auditor General's initiative, evaluation was only carried out on a small number of externally funded projects, by few agencies, in an ad hoc manner.

In Indonesia, while the World Bank since the early 1990s had been raising the issue of evaluation capacity in the context of the normal conduct of business, leadership calling for institutionalization came from a senior adviser to the President, who persuaded the National Development Planning Agency (BAPPENAS) to carry out an institutional diagnosis, leading to a proposal for setting up an evaluation system. The stated rationale for taking the step was that Indonesia's new development plan—REPELITA VI—needed to be concerned much more with equity and social issues. The government felt that, in the face of growing demand for public resources and services, evaluation could help increase their productivity and minimize waste. In 1994, an institutional diagnosis was started and in 1996 a proposal for evaluation capacity development was endorsed by BAPPENAS (Barbarie 1995). Based partly on the Chinese experience, BAPPENAS assembled a multi-agency steering group to provide direction for the institutional diagnosis. The diagnosis itself was carried out by national and international experts. To address the legal underpinning of the evaluation function and clarify incentives, the final proposal included, on one hand, drafting of a ministerial decree formally outlining the responsibilities of the various agencies in the evaluation system, and on the other, more closely linking the annual resource allocation process with performance monitoring and evaluation results. The Ministerial decree was formally issued in late 1996.

As Toulemonde suggests in chapter 7, demand for evaluation does not arise spontaneously, it must be nurtured through appropriate incentives and leadership. Laws and regulations are a necessary part of the incentives framework, but not a sufficient condition for a successful institutionalization of evaluation. The three country cases described here provide evidence of a varied set of conditions and circumstances. The successful implementation of an evaluation regime requires an enabling environment, that is, where there are real pressures for the type of institutional change that systematic public sector evaluation represents. The pressures can be external, driven by public account-ability demands, or accountability to, for example, external funding agencies. The pressures can be internal, to meet laws, rules and regula-tions, or to meet managerial needs. The pressures can also arise from resource constraints. As Derlien (1990) has shown, these conditions have a clear parallel in the development of evaluation in industrial countries. But, institutionalizing evaluation also requires direction and leadership, that is, a champion with power and commitment to build consensus and make the necessary decisions. As will be discussed be-low, an evaluation system must also be feasible, that is, capable of implementation through actionable steps by skilled staff and financial resources . Finally, the incentives framework must include effective rewards for those who are called to either produce or use evaluation, or be responsible for evaluation outcomes.

Organizing the Evaluation Function

There are at least three aspects related to the organization of evalua-tion. In chapters 1 and 2, Mayne, Divorski, and Lemaire and Sonnichsen discussed salient lessons on location of the evaluation function drawn from industrial country experience. These lessons address whether the evaluation function in the public sector should be in the executive branch or in the legislative; whether it should be centralized or decentralized; and whether to develop internal evaluation expertise or utilize outside experts. Bastoe in chapter 4 has also discussed the linkages of evalua-tion to other key public sector functions, and its implications for orga-nization of the function. How have Colombia, China, and Indonesia addressed these organizational aspects?

In Colombia, the 1991 Constitution calls on the executive to lead the process of institutionalizing the evaluation function in the public sec-tor. It also calls on the Controller General to independently carry out performance and compliance audits. The National Planning Depart-ment (NPD) is directed to implement the new constitutional mandate. It is doing so by linking evaluation to the National Development Plan, involving key government agencies responsible for implementing pub-lic expenditure programs (The World Bank 1997). These agencies must prepare annual plans specifying expected outputs, outcomes and per-formance measures, which will serve as a basis for ongoing and ex post evaluation of public sector performance. The planning units of each agency are responsible for the annual ex post evaluation activities and for delivering such evaluations to the NPD as a prerequisite for budget allocation requests. The NPD plans to conduct selected in depth ex post evaluations of policies, sectors, programs, or entities, which it will use as a basis for defining the subsequent expenditure program, identify institutional needs, and review strategic policy formulation. In addition, inter agency coordination units will bring together representatives of relevant stakeholders, including ministries, implementing agencies, departments and municipalities, and the civil sector. These units will provide coordination, cross-entity planning and evaluation oversight. To address the increasing demand for accountability, the proposed system also calls for the Controller General to check periodically on data quality and collection procedures.

In China, the evaluation system is being institutionalized following a decentralized approach. While the State Planning Commission is entrusted by the State Council to issue the regulations and to commission evaluation of public sector programs, evaluation units have developed in key central agencies. For example, the State Development Bank, Ministry of Construction, the China Engineering Consulting Corporation—a technical arm of the State Planning Commission, and others have set up evaluation units. In all these cases, the evaluation units are being located at the highest levels of each organization, to ensure independence from operational line responsibilities. The ministerial proposal for the evaluation system mentioned earlier calls for decentralizing evaluation responsibilities to provincial public sector agencies. It also calls on the State Audit Administration to provide oversight of the evaluation system. In China, there are no formal links yet established to ensure that evaluation information is fed to other key government functions, such as public expenditure allocations. However, the infrastructure for such links is being set up. At this early stage of the institutionalization process, China is putting greater effort into using evaluation information as a learning function, and to improve agency management of public sector programs.

In Indonesia, the organization of the evaluation function in the public sector is following a path similar to Colombia's. Evaluation is seen as a tool to correct policy and public expenditure programs, through more direct linkages to the National Development Plan and the resource allocation processes. Specifically, the Indonesian evaluation system relies on strengthening evaluation in all the key central and decentralized government agencies, with BAPPENAS at the apex. The proposal under implementation calls for strengthening monitoring and performance measurement in the line units within each agency, coupled with the establishment of units independent from the line at the top of each agency. The function of these units is to ensure that all public expenditures have appropriate monitoring mechanisms, and that the information is evaluated at the agency strategic level. These units then feed the relevant evaluation information to BAPPENAS to support the annual budget request cycle. BAPPENAS, which is a powerful resource allocation agency, will also strengthen its own evaluation capabilities to provide cross-sectoral and strategic evaluations to the top policy makers, and to facilitate adjustment to the development plans. The Indonesian evaluation institutionalization plan calls for an eventual oversight role for the internal and external audit agencies. This will come in due course when the audit agencies have been sufficiently strengthened to meet this responsibility.

As Mayne, Divorski, and Lemaire suggest in chapter 1, for evaluation to be successfully implemented—and it is still too early to tell in the three cases presented here—it must be located in several places within the governance structure if its to meet the demands of the various markets and stakeholders. In both Colombia and Indonesia, the organization of evaluation in the public sector has been driven by an explicit expression of information needs from the demand side. In these two cases, the demand has come from the well expressed decision of the powerful national planning agencies to link evaluation information to resource allocation processes. However, in all three countries, the impetus for evaluation institutionalization is lodged in the executive where, as Mayne, Divorski, and Lemaire argue, the relevance of government programs is unlikely to be challenged. As these systems mature, these countries are likely to experience an increasing need to strengthen the oversight role of independent agencies reporting to the legislative. Indeed, in the case of Colombia, the role of Controller General in evaluation is recognized in the new constitution. In China, the Auditor General, who played a pivotal role in the beginning of the evaluation institutionalization process, may as contemplated in the proposal before the State Council eventually take up specific responsibilities regarding oversight of the performance of the evaluation system. In Indonesia, the situation is similar to that of China, although the Auditor General's office participated in the process of setting up an evaluation system, it has not played an active part in defining its own role. In this respect, industrial country experience, such as the case of Australia, provides useful models of interaction between the executive and legislative, with regards to the role of the independent audit agency (Mackay, 1996).

Complementing the above considerations, the three governments recognize the importance of both locating evaluation with program management, tied to expenditure implementation within agencies, and locating evaluation at the corporate level in the form of evaluation units separated from operational responsibilities, and reporting independently to agency management. Similarly, in Colombia and Indonesia an important aim is to decentralize evaluation responsibilities to all actors with public expenditure allocation responsibilities. It is important to note in this regard that Colombia and Indonesia are implementing fiscal decentralization policies. China is de facto decentralizing, and is equally concerned with extending evaluation responsibilities over time to all relevant public sector agencies, central and decentralized. A decentralized evaluation function with clear reporting responsibilities is a natural complement to the decentralization process itself. In other words, if a key objective of decentralization is to bring decision making closer to the clients of public services, only a decentralized results based evaluation process, for example at the local government level, will ensure that adequate signals are generated about whether welfare enhancing results are being attained. Often the local political process itself is supposed to assure feedback and improved accountability, but still, without transparent information on outcomes through systematic evaluation processes, it is naive to believe that decentralized public expenditures will yield desired results.

Supply Considerations

The most relevant spectrum of evaluation activities in developing countries ranges from policy, at the strategic and sectoral levels, to public expenditure programs, and to investment projects. This range of evaluation coverage defines the questions that evaluation must answer. These questions in turn determine the supply requirements. Broadly, resources required to carry out evaluations fall into four generally interdependent categories: methods and standards, information, financial resources, and professional skills. Information resources are largely determined by the specific evaluation methodologies to be used to answer the evaluation . But, the methods themselves depend on the evaluation questions to be answered, the financial resources, skills, and time available for evaluation. Evaluation timing is also key to meeting demand (Chelimsky, 1987) which often leads to tradeoffs among these supply factors. For example, the best methodology may also be the most resource intensive and the one that would take the longest to yield the information demanded. If evaluations are not produced in time to be responsive to demand, resources committed to it will be questioned and support for the function will wane.

In all three countries, the above inputs are in constrained supply; but while financial and information resources are limited, the more severe shortages are in the methodological and skills areas. Boyle in chapter 6, as well as Bemelmans-Videc (1992) discuss in detail the human resource development issues involved in effective evaluation practice. While evaluation methods for program and project evaluation are well-developed and known in industrial countries, methods for the evaluation of public policies are continuously evolving. Newer areas such as methods for the evaluation of policy advice are beginning to be developed and put into practice (Uhr and Mackay 1996). While in all three countries there are academic programs to train professionals in the social and technical sciences, in none are there programs in evaluation. Evaluation, to the extent that it is practiced, is carried out by professionals trained in other disciplines. Indeed, evaluation per se is not seen as a profession; rather it is seen as a transdiscipline tapping multidisciplinary skills. All three countries have, nevertheless, been sending prospective evaluation staff for training abroad, or inviting foreign lecturers to train local officials and professionals in evaluation methods. All three countries have also considered setting professional evaluation standards, with China and Indonesia having drafted specific proposals. China and Indonesia are also encouraging their academic community to get involved in evaluation. Indeed, in these two countries, local universities participated actively in the institutional assessments made prior to the launching of the function. China is taking this one step beyond by also pursuing the establishment of an evaluation professional association bringing together the official sector, local universities and research institutions, as well as external experts.

In the case of Indonesia, the evaluation system being put in place also calls for training in evaluation for different levels. It calls for training in technical skills for evaluators, interpersonal skills to encourage a multidisciplinary evaluation approach, and management skills, for those who are put in charge of the evaluation units in the various agencies.

Indonesia, as well as China, are also considering filling the skills gap by commissioning outside parties to carry out evaluation. Indonesia proposes to encourage the use of third parties when specialized expertise is needed, but also to fill gaps and enhance independence. In general, evaluation is not yet seen as a career in the public services. Due to lack of experience, evaluation is seen with caution. Those who champion evaluation do not have doubts about the implications of developing a strong function. But, public officials called upon to undertake evaluation responsibilities express concern about their professional careers; they often see a risk that their work will be seen as a conveyer of bad news. This is not an untypical reaction of evaluation practitioners everywhere. In the three countries reviewed here, as well as other developing countries taking steps to institutionalize the evaluation function, it is amply recognized that evaluation as an institution of governance will succeed when an evaluation culture has been established. For evaluation to take root as a profession it will be necessary to do what, for example, Australia or New Zealand are aiming to accomplish in terms of creating such an evaluation culture in government at all levels. Prior chapters, such as Toulemondes', suggest that developing an evaluation culture is a long-term process of building the incentives as well as capacity.

On information requirements, Colombia and Indonesia aim to identify monitoring and performance indicators to be used in the tracking and evaluation of public expenditure programs. Yet, in none of these cases are the information systems in place to do so. China has a well developed system of information requirements mostly designed to track the implementation of public sector programs. All three countries are taking steps to complement their existing information systems with data requirements focusing on intermediate outcomes and results. This is also a long-term process which involves building the information infrastructure in parallel with the development of the evaluation function. In none of these three cases has the ready availability of information been seen as a precondition to institutionalize evaluation

On the financial resource side, in all three countries evaluation is seen as a mainstream function of each public agency, and not an add-on unfunded responsibility. In China and Indonesia, evaluation is to be funded from the regular budgets of the public sector agencies. There are no separate budgets being considered to provide financial incentives for evaluation. In Colombia, the budget is to provide a more strategic support for results oriented public resource allocations. As already indicated, in Colombia, budget submissions should be underpinned by evaluation information.

Bridging Demand and Supply

The relatively recent history of evaluation capacity development in developing countries, including that of Colombia, China, and Indonesia, and the experience of industrialized countries reported in this book, confirms the major findings of the previously cited World Bank task force report on the subject. These findings are worth synthesizing:

- Evaluation is a long-term, difficult, and complex proposition. Nurturing genuine demand for evaluation of the effectiveness of public actions and the need to build ownership are the pivotal steps in most countries. The three country cases discussed amply illustrate this emphasis.
- Evaluation capacity development must be treated as an integral part of efforts to improve public sector reform and institutional development. Using different instruments and approaches, the three countries have sought to develop evaluation as a mainstream function, and not a separate isolated institution.
- The focus of evaluation capacity development interventions should depend on the institutional conditions of the country in question. In all three cases, the institutional framework is different and the evaluation approaches followed have been tailored to meet the particular requirements. While each country has been keen to learn about the experience of others, this has not been with the intention to transfer approaches, but to adapt best practice to the local conditions and constraints.
- Information must be adequate for effective evaluation and must be accessible to those who need to use it. All three countries recognize the need for adequate information and have set up the mechanisms to begin to develop responsive information systems. While the information systems are developed, these countries are introducing ad-hoc information gathering approaches.
- Where past evaluation capacity development efforts have not yielded satisfactory results, the most common reason is that they were seen as externally driven, with limited country participation, and too modest to have a critical mass. In all three cases, while the World Bank has taken steps to help promote the institutionalization of evaluation, the focus of the effort has not been on externally funded programs and projects, but public expenditure at large and driven by local needs.
- The demand for and country ownership of evaluation can best be developed if it is seen as a vehicle earning and improving future performance, not just as an accountability instrument. The institutional assessments that have preceded the institutionalization of evaluation have led to recommendations encouraging appropriate checks and balances, not only within pub-

lic agencies, but among agencies. In all these cases, the trends is to strengthen line as well as apex evaluation within agencies. In all three cases, evaluation in the executive agencies of government are complemented by strengthening of the oversight function of independent agencies, such as auditor generals or controller not reporting to the executive.

As seen in the three country cases, to successfully bridge the demand and supply conditions affecting evaluation capacity development interventions required an in-depth diagnosis of a country's institutional framework. From this diagnosis realistic proposals were made about institutionalizing evaluation capacity and its pace. The diagnostic studies provided a forum to develop and nurture demand and political support for evaluation. They helped point to areas where supply capacity needed improvement, such as in building skills and information infrastructure. They also helped identify how external support could be best utilized.

Table 8.2 illustrates more specific options in evaluation capacity development in response to different demand and supply conditions, using the framework outlined in the Introduction. Since there is no unique evaluation capacity development strategy that is appropriate for all countries, flexible and opportunistic approaches may work best. The interventions listed in the table are only suggestions and are not to be treated either as an exhaustive list nor as rigid prescriptions. Indeed, in each country there are likely to be present, like in the cases reviewed in this paper, both weak and strong features on both the demand and supply side. The framework only highlights the case for analyzing each intervention against demand and supply conditions so as to match the evaluation capacity development strategy to the country context. The approach underscores the need to differentiate between countries and to adopt a graduated evaluation capacity development strategy.

The mix of interventions will depend on the priority the evaluation function is to be given in the public sector management reform in each country. The evaluation capacity development interventions derived from the above analysis should be matched with a country's ongoing or proposed public sector management reforms. These reforms should provide a basis for deciding the priority, mix and timing of the interventions. For example, in countries where both demand and supply conditions are weak, it may be premature to think about locating the evaluation function in any part of government. In developing countries with important funding from external agencies, it might be more appropriate to initiate joint evaluation of specific projects and programs as a catalyst for further development. This is not to deny the importance of a focal point for evaluation to provide national leadership.

But, it might be prudent to be experimental and learn rather than to be dogmatic about the evaluation location issue. In general, the evaluation capacity development process should evolve in the direction of strong demand and supply. The road to get there may be circuitous.

In Conclusion

The earlier discussion of demand and supply issues in Colombia, China, and Indonesia show how the above framework can be used to take stock and assess the conditions in any country. There is no need to repeat how these countries match the framework, but a few points are worth highlighting:

- In China and Indonesia, it was deemed appropriate to begin the evaluation capacity development process with an institutional diagnosis;
- In all three countries, there was an expressed need to raise awareness among key decision makers;
- In all three cases, the was a keen interest by the local authorities to learn about international experience, particularly about promising approaches to evaluation capacity development;
- Colombia has commissioned independent evaluation of important projects, while the capacity is being developed and mainstreamed;
- In China and Indonesia, there has been a great interest in participating more actively in the evaluations carried out by external funding agencies, such as the World Bank;
- On the other hand, in Colombia and Indonesia there is a policy decision to link evaluation to the key functions of government, e.g. strategic planning and resource allocation;
- China and Indonesia are also taking steps to strengthen the capacity of independent oversight agencies outside the executive;
- Colombia is actively promoting the dissemination of evaluation results to the public.

In short, broad steps are being taken in these countries to address weak demand and supply areas, but progress and interest is not limited to these. In a sense, having made the decision to institutionalize evaluation in government, authorities are impatient to adopt or put in place evaluation mechanisms and procedures more akin to those being set up in industrial countries. These, and other developing countries embarked on strengthening their evaluation capacities as part of their public sector reform programs, are intent on bypassing the waves (Derlien, 1990) that have characterized the ups and downs of evaluation in industrial

TABLE 8.2
Evaluation Capacity Development Framework for Action

Demand

		Strong	Weak
Supply	Strong	■ Support evaluation of policies, programs and projects ■ Establish links between evaluation, strategic, planning, resource allocation, and budgets ■ Use expert commissions to evaluate policies ■ Strengthen evaluation in the legislature ■ Disseminate evaluation results to the public ■ Organize and systematize the evaluation function ■ Support financial and information systems	■ Disseminate evaluation methods and practices ■ Support ongoing evaluation of programs and projects ■ Participate in evaluations done by external funding agencies ■ Support professional development in evaluation ■ Support research institutions in carrying out evaluation
	Weak	■ Disseminate lessons of experience and best practices ■ Set up commissions to evaluate important projects or programs ■ Train and use private sector institutions in evaluations ■ Support university training in evaluation ■ Provide technical assistance to government agencies ■ Build evaluation network within government ■ Promote evaluation by non-government agencies ■ Introduce evaluation standards	■ Strengthen audit and accounting ■ Carry out joint evaluations with funding agencies ■ Disseminate national and international lessons of experience ■ Support evaluation training in educational institutions ■ Carry out country institutional and evaluation capacity assessments ■ Promote cross-country co-operation in evaluation ■ Raise awareness among decision makers

countries, and move to adopt more robust and sustainable approaches based on what works.

References

Barbarie, A. 1995. "Strengthening Performance Evaluation Capacity." Unpublished report prepared for the National Development Planning Agency, Republic of Indonesia, Jakarta.

Bates, R.H. 1995. "Social Dilemmas and Rational Individuals—An assessment of the new institutionalism." In J. Harriss, J. Hunter, and C.L. Lewis (eds.), *The New Institutional Economics and Third World Development*, New York : Routledge.

Bemelmans-Videc, M.L. 1992. "Institutionalizing Evaluation: International Perspectives." In J. Mayne et al. (eds.), *Advancing Public Policy Evaluation: Learning from International Experiences*, New York: North-Holland.

Chelimsky, E. 1987. "What have we learned about the Politics of Program Evaluation." *Evaluation Practice*, Volume 8, Number 1, February 1987, Sage Publications.

Departamento Nacional de Planeacion. 1992. *Control y Evaluacion de la Gestion Publica—Los Desafios de la Nueva Constitucion*. Santafe de Bogota: DNP.

Derlien, H-U. 1990. "Genesis and Structure of Evaluation Efforts in Comparative Perspective." In R.C. Rist (ed.), *Program Evaluation and the Management of Government—Patterns & Prospects across Eight Nations*. New Brunswick, NJ: Transactions Publishers.

Havens, Harry S. 1992. "The Erosion of Federal Program Evaluation." In C.G. Wye and R.C. Sonnichsen (eds.), *Evaluation in the Federal Government: Changes, Trends, and Opportunities*. New Directions for Program Evaluation, Number 55, Fall 1992, Jossey-Bass Publishers.

Hong, H. and R.C. Rist. 1997. "The Development of Evaluation in the People's Republic of China." In E. Chelimsky and W.R. Shadish (eds.), *Evaluation for the 21st Century—A Handbook*. Thousand Oaks: Sage Publications.

Khan, M.A. 1994. "Establishing a Performance Evaluation Capacity in the Public Sector of the People's Republic of China." Unpublished report prepared for the World Bank Department, Ministry of Finance, Beijing.

Mackay, K. 1996. "The Institutional Framework for Evaluation in the Australian Government." Paper delivered to a World Bank seminar, Department of Finance, Canberra.

Stiglitz, J.E. 1989. "On the Economic Role of the State." In A. Heertje (ed.), *The Economic Role of the State*. London: Basil Blackwell.

Stiglitz, J.E. 1994. *Whither Socialism*. Massachusetts: The MIT Press.

The World Bank. 1994. *Report of the Evaluation Capacity Development Task Force*. Washington, DC: The World Bank.

The World Bank. 1997. *Colombia—Paving the Way for a Results-Oriented Public Sector*. Washington, D.C.: The World Bank.

Uhr, J. and K. Mackay. 1996. *Evaluating Policy Advice: Learning from Commonwealth Experience*. Federalism Research Centre, Australian National University, Canberra.

Wiesner, E.D. 1993. *From Macroeconomic Correction to Public Sector Reform—The Critical Role of Evaluation*. World Bank Discussion Paper No. 214. Washington, D.C: The World Bank.

Wiesner, E.D. 1997. "Evaluation, Markets and Institutions in the Reform Agenda of Developing Countries." In E. Chelimsky and W.R. Shadish (eds.), *Evaluation for the 21st Century—A Handbook*. Thousand Oaks: Sage Publications.

Postscript: Evaluation Capacity Building— A Journey without an End

Donald Lemaire and Richard Boyle

The purpose of this postscript is to briefly revisit some of the issues outlined throughout the book and to add a few remaining comments for thought and future exploration.

Evaluation is a well-documented process. Indeed, there are many books and articles that describe both how evaluation results are used and also how evaluation techniques expand our capacity to assess what results government activities achieve. What has been the focus of less attention and scrutiny is the institutionalization of the discipline of evaluation and the building of an ongoing evaluation capacity. The purpose of this book has been to provide an overview and reference work that describes the application of lessons learned in the public sector. For instance, Guerrero, in chapter 8, applies the lessons learned to the experience in developing countries.

The practice of enshrining the evaluation process both as a key function and as a tool of good governance within public sector organizations presents a significant challenge to governments and bureaucrats alike. Experience in industrial countries shows that each country has unique institutional characteristics which make generalizations difficult, inadvisable, or very risky. Institutional arrangements affect what can be expected from evaluation; they influence the focus of evaluation, its links to decisionmaking and administration and its overall status. This in turn affects who is interested in the issues addressed, who has access to the information, and who finds the results credible and worth using.

There are four key themes that emerge from the work of the various contributors to this book which should be of assistance to those involved in the institutionalization of evaluation as part of the governance process. The first is the importance of balance—balance between the demand for and the supply of evaluation capacity. As Mayne, Divorski, and Lemaire show in chapter 1, this involves understanding three things: first, that there are multiple demands and markets for evaluation; second, that in anchoring the evaluation regime, thought needs to be given to the needs of these various markets; and third, that priorities must be set to meet the needs of governance at any particular moment in time.

The second theme addressed by contributors relates to the need to be flexible and to utilize opportunities and incentives to foster evaluation capacity development. This is most explicitly addressed by Toulemonde (chap. 7) when he looks at the role of incentives, constraints, and culture building (or "carrots, sticks, and sermons," as he alternatively calls them) in developing evaluation demand. Looking at a range of examples of successful institutionalization of evaluation, he shows how a mix of incentives are needed to foster evaluation demand. Such incentives include budgetary and career incentives. But he also illustrates that incentives on their own are not enough. They need to be complemented by appropriate constraints and the development of a culture in the public service that accepts and supports evaluation activity.

The existence of multiple markets for evaluation provides opportunities for evaluation capacity to be developed at more than one level or location. And, while there is no a priori specific location and level to initiate evaluation capacity building, such opportunities should not be addressed in an ad hoc manner. Opportunism needs to be tempered with an understanding of the complexity of the evaluation markets, and within a thought-through strategic approach to evaluation institutionalization, as illustrated by the successful experiences highlighted in this book. Lee (chap. 3) indicates how Australia and Canada put a strong emphasis on systematically integrating evaluation into corporate and program management and planning, as part of broad public service reforms. There is also strong central ministry coordination and encouragement of evaluation. Toulemonde (chap. 7) shows how in the Netherlands, the Reconsideration of Public Expenditure system was tailored to suit the prevailing administrative culture. As a result, it had some considerable degree of success.

This brings us to the third key theme, which relates to the actual governmental approaches being used to enhance the demand for evaluation and the need for resilience. In trying to develop supply and demand, governments have had more experience with using a supply-push approach. Indeed we began in the introduction to this book by noting that in many countries there is often weak demand for evaluation. Rist addresses this issue in chapter 5, where he examines appropriate ways to link what he calls the disparate worlds of political systems and evaluation systems. He looks at how evaluation can be linked to decision-making at the various stages in the policy cycle, and also how to promote governmental and organizational learning through evaluation practice. This conceptual use of evaluation to enhance learning can foster a positive cycle of further development of evaluation practice and subsequent utilization of evaluations.

A strategic approach requires flexibility to intervene on the supply side in parallel with the demand side. Sonnichsen (chap. 2) and Boyle (chap. 6) both note how interventions on the supply side can help ensure an appropriate match between supply and demand. Sonnichsen explores the relative advantages and disadvantages of using evaluators employed full time in an organization or of using expertise bought in from outside, or some combination of these two. He also explores the relative benefits of centralizing or decentralizing evaluation within organizations. Boyle identifies a mix of strategies that governments may use and which are appropriate to the professionalization of the evaluation function.

In essence, what is needed is an approach that recognizes the complexity of demand for evaluation, promotes coherent demand strategies, and adjusts supply strategies accordingly. The first and second wave of evaluation regime development mentioned in the introduction indicate the importance of supply strategies that are responsive to demand. In the first wave, demand was led by a desire to improve government programs. In the second wave, public accountability and budgetary restrictions led the demand for evaluation activities. Supply must respond to such changing demands if demand is to be self-sustaining and effective over more than the short term. In this, evaluation is no different than other key public sector functions. Budgeting, strategic planning, audit, and performance monitoring functions continue to evolve and adjust to a constant changing environment. These functions are an integral part of the learning process of public sector organizations.

The fourth theme that emerged is the mainstreaming of evaluation regimes into the functions of government. Good governance requires meaningful accountability, both at the political and the administrative levels. A public sector based on transparency, probity, management systems that are efficient and effective in determining priorities, the allocation of resources in line with these priorities, and assessment of the extent to which objectives related to priorities are met, provides a sound foundation for meaningful accountability. The management tools available to public sector management have made substantial progress in meeting these requirements. Financial management systems provide for transparency and probity in accounting for public spending. Key public management functions such as budgeting, strategic planning, audit, and performance monitoring continue to evolve in providing the information necessary for meaningful accountability.

These public sector management functions serve specific purposes and have their own *raison d'être*. However, as the old adage says, the whole is bigger than the sum of the parts. Bastoe (chap. 4) looks at how evaluation links with these other public sector functions, and under what conditions a coherent integrated performance management system can be achieved. For demand to be strong and effective requires links to be developed within and between the different markets for evaluation and the different public sector functions.

In conclusion, the analogy of evaluation "waves" referred to in the introduction is most pertinent to building evaluation capacity. Evaluation capacity development and the institutionalization of evaluation are not one-time events. Countries, and different government levels within countries, have witnessed phases of expansion and contraction of their evaluation capacity. Factors influencing such waves of development are only beginning to be observed and explored. We need to understand these factors if governments are to be able, in the words of Picciotto in his foreword to this volume, to develop the "design criteria needed to build resilient evaluation systems." *Resilience* is a key word here. If evaluation is to be effectively institutionalized, it must be resilient to withstand the changing pressures of public governance. *Flexibility* is another key word. Evaluation regimes must be flexible to meet the varying demands from the multiple markets which exist for evaluation. The central challenge for those involved in developing evaluation capacity in government today is how to get the balance right between the supply of and demand for evaluation, and how to mix resilience and flexibility within the system. The lessons learned and the comparative experiences illustrated in this book give some guidance as to how to achieve such a balance.

Contributors

Per Oyvind Bastoe is senior evaluation officer in the Operations Evaluation Department in the World Bank's headquarters in Washington, DC. He has previously been researcher/assistant professor, and has had senior positions in the Norwegian government administration, including director of the Analysis Department in the Directorate of Public Management. He has published several books, articles, and reports on organizational development, result-based management, evaluation, planning, and social policy.

Richard Boyle is senior research officer with the Institute of Public Administration in Ireland. Before joining the Institute in 1986, he worked in the local government service in England on policy review and evaluation. His work focuses on public service reform, managing for results in the public service and developing and implementing effective performance management systems. He has published numerous books and articles on program evaluation and performance measurement.

R. Pablo Guerrero is an economist with the World Bank in Washington, DC. Since January 1998 he is partnerships coordinator in the Strategy and Resource Management vice-presidency. Prior to taking up this post he was adviser to the Director General Operations Evaluation. Before joining the World Bank, he was chief of operations evaluation at the Inter-American Development Bank. His current work focuses on partnerships, within developing countries and between them and development funding agencies, as instruments to enhance development effectiveness. He has also spearheaded efforts in the development community to help strengthen evaluation capacity in developing countries.

Donald Lemaire is director, Alternative Service Delivery, Service and Innovation Sector, Treasury Board of Canada Secretariat. He previously served as General Counsel, Department of Justice Canada, from 1993–1998. He also worked at the Office of the Comptroller General and at Correctional Services Canada. Mr. Lemaire holds a B.Sci. Soc. (1979), Université d'Ottawa; M.A. en économie (1980), Université d'Ottawa; L.L.L. (1983), Université d'Ottawa; Barreau du Québec (1984); D.E.A. (1988), Laboratoire d'économie et de sociologie du travail, Aix-en-Provence, France.

John Mayne is currently a principal with the Office of the Auditor General, where he is responsible for the audit areas of accountability, alternative service delivery, and implementing enhanced performance measurement and reporting. He work previously in Treasury Board Secretariat and the Office of the Comptroller General, where he was instrumental in the development of the federal government's approach to evaluating programs. In recent years, Dr. Mayne has been leading efforts at developing effective performance measurement and reporting practices in the government of Canada. He has authored numerous articles, reports, and books in the areas of program evaluation, public administration, and performance monitoring.

Ray C. Rist is the evaluation advisor to the Economic Development Institute of the World Bank. He has held prior academic appointments at Cornell University, Johns Hopkins University, and George Washington University. He also has had senior appointments in both the legislative and executive branches of the United States government. Dr. Rist has authored or edited twenty-four books, written more than 125 articles, and lectured in nearly fifty countries. He has been a senior Fulbright fellow in Germany and has also received the Medal of Merit from the Parliament of France.

Richard Sonnichsen is a retired FBI agent and currently an evaluation and management consultant. His main interest is the development of internal evaluation functions in organizations and he is writing a book on how this can be successfully accomplished. He has a doctorate in Public Administration and has taught at the University of Southern California, Washington Public Affairs Center in Washington, D. C. He lives with his wife Sally, in Sandpoint, Idaho.

Jacques Toulemonde, is scientific director and co-founder of the Centre for European Evaluation Expertise (C3E) where he co-ordinates a program on evaluation methods in the field of European structural funds (MEANS). He has previously served on a committee of experts responsible for auditing the European Commission's evaluation practices, at the request of the Directorate General XIX (Budgets), and is currently a member of the editorial advisory board of the journal Knowledge and Policy. He is the author and editor of articles and books dealing with the institutionialization and professionalization of evaluation, evaluation in partnership, causality analysis, and evaluation techniques.

Yoon-Shik Lee is professor and chairman at the Department of Public Administration of Soong Sil University in Seoul, Korea. He has published articles, monographs, and reports on public administration and program evaluation, and has done comparative work in the area of public administration between Korea and the U.S. He was visiting guest professor at the University of Maryland in 1995–96.

Index